THE GEEZERS' GUIDE TO FOOTBALL

D1341302

AUTHOR'S ACKNOWLEDGEMENTS

This book would not have been possible without the love and support of my wife, Tina, and my kids, Rebecca, Kayleigh and Ben.

Thanks are due to Bill and Cathy at Mainstream, Andy Smith and Steve Kingsman at CTX, Alistair McCloy, and also to Kevin Thorpe, the bloke in the wig on the cover.

This book was written on a Pentium II computer supplied by CTX Europe Ltd (01923 810800).

MAINSTREAM   *SPORT*

THE GEEZERS' GUIDE

TO FOOTBALL

A LIFETIME OF LADS AND LAGER

DOUGIE BRIMSON

MAINSTREAM
PUBLISHING

EDINBURGH AND LONDON

First published in Great Britain in 1998 by
MAINSTREAM PUBLISHING COMPANY (EDINBURGH) LTD
7 Albany Street
Edinburgh EH1 3UG

Reprinted 1999, 2000, 2001

ISBN 1 84018 114 1

A catalogue record for this book is available from the British Library

Typeset in Garamond
Printed and bound by
Cox & Wyman Ltd, Reading, Berkshire

Contents

Foreword

Over the last few years, the trickle of books dealing with the great game we call football has turned into a tidal wave of print. The days of searching around for something half decent to read in some dark, dusty corner of the local high-street bookshop or between the shrink-wrapped porno magazines in motorway service stations miles from anywhere have thankfully gone for ever. These days, the footie sections are positively bulging with reading material, and long may that remain the case.

Reluctant as I am to do it, I suppose I have to take some of the credit (or blame) for that. I have, after all, forged a career of sorts writing books with my younger brother Eddy about the realities of football hooliganism and the terrace culture we grew up with. There are now four paperbacks bearing our moniker on the bookshelves of Britain and thankfully they have all been moderately successful, enough to ensure that they will haunt the shelves of WH Smiths and the local libraries for some time to come. But we weren't alone by any means. Oh no. From the autobiographies of has-been (or wish-they-had-been) players and managers to in-depth examinations of the financial wheelings and dealings (not to mention failures) surrounding football, every aspect of the greatest sport the world has ever known has been covered and re-covered. Almost.

You see, whilst there have been thousands of books looking at football, there have been very few that have actually looked at that much-maligned creature, the supporter. There have been some, of course, and a few of these have passed into the 'classic, must read, must have' category – *Fever Pitch* and *This Supporting Life* are two that spring to mind. These two books in particular achieved that all too rare feat of capturing the spirit of football fandom and getting it on to the printed page in a way that captured the essence of the whole obsession perfectly. Indeed, one of the great strengths of *Fever Pitch* was that in almost every paragraph you could see either yourself or someone you knew.

Sadly, there are very few books that come even close to *Fever Pitch* and, in truth, I doubt we will ever see another like it. Generally speaking, most books that profess to deal with football fans have been non-fiction and have tended to concentrate on specific issues such as 'wimmin' supporters (*sic*) or hooliganism, and are either brilliant (and no prizes for guessing whose I mean by that) or crap (ditto). Either that or they have been diaries of specific seasons at specific clubs and hold little or no interest for anyone other than the supporters of that particular team. That isn't to decry them in any way. Far from it. But as a Watford fan, a book about Man United, West Ham or Hamilton Academical has no relevance to me and therefore I couldn't give a shit about it. Sorry and all that. But that's the way it is.

With the exception of the aforementioned *Fever Pitch*, much the same can be said about those novels written about the game because, as far as I'm concerned, they are all the same. And they are all crap. Think about it for a minute: boy goes to football, has fight, goes home, gets depressed, hates job, hates family, hates police, hates everyone else, hates fighting but can't stop, gets into drugs, etc., etc. The basis for almost every single novel released in recent years. Why is it that the only person who can write a novel about football without hooliganism being an integral element is Nick Hornby? Isn't there more to football-supporting than rucking? And yes, I am aware of the huge amount of irony contained in that statement thank you.

However, I digress. You see whilst almost every issue surrounding the game has been immortalised in print at some time or another, and supporters as a whole have received some, if not that much, attention, there is one specific group of fans who have never received the exposure they deserve, and this book aims to redress that appalling oversight. After all, it isn't even as if this is a minority group. In actual fact, it's the majority. Walk around any ground on the day of a match or stand outside the turnstile just after the final whistle has blown and you will see them in their thousands. In between the anoraks, old gits, 'wimmin' and kids there they will be: geezers. Bloody thousands of them. The one single group above all others that the professional game relies on, not only for income but to create that most important of things: atmosphere. Without them, professional football as an occasion would die overnight and it bloody well knows it.

Well, this book is about them and, to be honest, about me. You see football isn't just about 90 minutes, it's about passion and, yes, if you like, about life. We men will do things under the umbrella of football fandom that we would never dream of doing in any other sphere of life, and within the pages that follow I will try and explain why. I will do that primarily in the hope that it will bring more understanding from those who will never be one of us but who condemn us anyway because of who and what we are. The type of people who think that abusing a player is a mortal sin and that stadium catering should be both tasty and nutritious.

But, as the title suggests, this book is, above all, a guide. And therefore within *The Geezers' Guide to Football* (henceforth known as *GTF*) I will attempt to teach the ways of the terrace to those 'wannabe' individuals who, through the delights of Sky Sports or corporate freebies, have recently discovered our great game. If you are one such individual, and have just realised that standing behind the goal with other men is for you but you're terrified of showing yourself up and looking like a complete tosser, then read on. Within these pages I will provide information and insight which will prove invaluable to you.

Yet, make no mistake, this book is, above everything else, about football. Not about the game itself, you understand, but about something much more important: the culture of the football terrace. Tragically the very last bastion of our once male-dominated culture to be found anywhere. An environment where boys can grow up and act like proper men. The last place where we males can scream, shout, abuse, swear, even cry if we like without feeling like some effeminate twat.

If it's political correctness you want, or if you're the type of person who thinks that females have as much right to walk into a football ground and stand on the home end as any male, you can piss off right now. This book is not for you. I make no apologies for saying that it's sexist, abusive, ageist and élitist. After all, it's for geezers. And that is the very first and most important lesson of all because, in a nutshell, being sexist, abusive, ageist and élitist is what being a geezer is all about.

Part One

The Introduction

Chapter One

What Is a Geezer?

Before we get too engrossed in the educational side of things, it is important that you understand what a geezer actually is. After all, if you are already a member of this exalted breed then you will know it, but if you're not you will need some guidance. If for no other reason than you will have to recognise your peers at some point or another if you're going to avoid looking like a geek and want to evade a slapping.

However, the first thing you need to recognise is that whilst everyone can aspire to geezerdom, not everyone can achieve it. Let's be clear here: if you are some kind of first division wanker during your normal working life, going to football one day per week is highly unlikely to change that, is it? No matter how hard you try. And I must stress, and you must accept, that there is only one sex that makes the grade here. Forget all talk of 'girl power' and sexual equality; to be a geezer you must be a bloke, and there are absolutely no exceptions to that. If there is such a beast as a geezer-bird then I have yet to meet it, and this phrase remains a derogatory term of the highest order, to be aimed primarily at ugly 'wimmin', overgrown tomboys and lesbians. This is a subject we will return to later.

So just what is a geezer? Well, it's quite uncomplicated, really. Forget all that old bollocks about 'new men', 'soft men' or 'lads'; a geezer is, to put it simply, a male of the species who has managed, through fair means or foul, to resist the oppressive influences of the female race. Confident and proud to the point of arrogance, a geezer will, above all, remain loyal to his sex, his mates and his chosen football club. There is much more to the actual culture of geezerdom than that, as you will discover, but you get the general idea.

For those who still need help, I suppose I should provide you with some examples – just to clarify things, you understand. After all, they do say that a picture paints a thousand words and there are enough men working in the media to provide suitable role models for any aspiring geezer. You would think that, wouldn't you, but actually there aren't. I mean, look at the men who work in television for a start.

If you do manage to find one that isn't effeminate (in itself a fairly tall order), think about what it is that they actually do. First, they get dressed by some butch bird from a costume department and then they are freshly made up (made up!) by some faggot. They then sit in front of a camera and read out things from an autocue, most, if not all, of which has been written by somebody else. Hardly the most masculine of occupations to be involved in. Even those who are held up as 'lads' fail the test. Take Jeremy Clarkson as a prime example. Leaving aside the fact that he went to public school (in itself a perfectly reasonable excuse for exclusion from geezerdom) and has a stupid haircut (ditto), he just comes across as a total tosser. He's no lad and he's certainly no geezer. He's what executives at the BBC and old ladies *think* is a lad. Which just goes to show how out of touch they really are.

To be fair, though, the telly has tried its best over the years to portray the average bloke in a positive light, but in the main the results have been pathetic. Look at *Men Behaving Badly* for a start. Supposedly the ultimate in geezer programming. But what is it that you have actually got? Two sad losers vainly trying to keep hold of their long-gone youth. One of them can only get a bird by grovelling and the other lets his rule the roost. What sort of role models are those two? They don't even seem to like football, for fuck's sake! *Game On* was another vain attempt at capturing the male character, but all we ended up with was another two sad blokes sharing a flat with a bird who, once again, ruled the roost. And, still, no football. Oh dear.

So let's move very swiftly on, shall we? What about those two off *Fantasy Football League*? Yeah, right-oh! Skinner and Baddiel, television's resident professional 'lads'. What a great pair these two are. At least Gary and Tony from *MBB* are acting; these two twats

seem to actually believe that they are the real thing. God help us!
If you think good old Frank and Dave are true geezers then think
again, mate. Liking football and drinking the odd bottle of beer
hardly makes you a lad, does it? I mean, some sort of masculinity
by-pass or even a testosterone injection might make a difference
to these two, but even that's doubtful. At least they have football
on, but that's nowhere near enough of a consolation. In any case,
they deserve to be excluded from the male race if for no other
reason than they were involved in the anoraks' anthem 'Three
Lions'. Still, they seem to be happy living their lives in luvvie-
land, so let's leave them there.

As football is the focus of our existence, then surely the game
should be able to help us out? Well, no actually. However, the
reason for football's failure to provide an example of geezerdom
has nothing to do with individuals. It is to do with personal
choice. I mean, as a Watford fan, I believe (I have to believe) that
anyone who doesn't play for Watford is, obviously, a wanker. You
may not necessarily agree with that and I will understand
perfectly if you insert your own team into the last sentence, but
the result should be the same. Indeed, I have absolutely no doubt
that the first-team squad at Vicarage Road would throw up a few
excellent examples for us to consider. But, sadly, I doubt they
would mean much to anyone foolish enough to follow another
side and so, in the spirit of fairness, I will press on. And before
you mention it, forget the national squad. As a footie fan, they
have to be strictly second choice behind your club side.

No, we need to look elsewhere for our role models, and rather
than examine players or so-called personalities, what about taking
a look at a few characters from the soaps? How about Phil and
Grant off *Eastenders*? Or someone from the Street, or anything
else, for that matter? Well no, I'm afraid not. After all, the Mitchell
boys' characters may be hard as nails but when was the last time
you saw them taking Saturday off to go and watch the Hammers?
And why isn't there a big-screen television in the Queen Vic so
that they can watch the Monday night footie? East-end boys? I
think not. At least up there on *Coronation Street* some of the lads
will occasionally go and watch that club they call 'City'. (And if it
really is, as most people suspect, *Manchester* City, why do they wear
green and white scarves every time anyone goes to a match? We
should be told.) But Curly wears glasses and is far too sad and

Martin is a nurse (enough said). Even Des Barnes (single, own house, bookie) fails the test because at the merest whiff of skirt he throws himself on the floor and turns into a doormat.

So the soaps are out. What else is there? What about the music business, then? Listen, if you think the words 'Oasis' and 'geezer' even belong in the same sentence then you should be taken out and shot. Being abusive, advocating drug abuse, getting drunk and trashing hotel rooms does not make you a geezer. It makes you a nobhead. A talented nobhead, granted, but still a nobhead. After all, excess is something no self-respecting geezer would ever contemplate. Except in a pub. In fact, let's not piss about. For that very reason, the music business and the media in general can be excluded because they are industries dependent on excess. Being a celebrity, by its very nature, means being false to some extent. They are individuals who are either manufactured or manipulated into a position of fame by others, a product of someone else's imagination or creative process – and that is hardly something to be proud of or respected for, is it? And for the geezer, that is the key word: respect.

You see, respect isn't a right, it's earned. The media manufacture people, push them out to us as role models and expect us to respect and admire them. Not for who they are, but for what they are. However, in the vast majority of cases, they are the very people we shouldn't admire at all because, generally speaking, they are tossers. After all, would you really want your son to have the personality of Paul Gascoigne or Jeremy Clarkson?

I am, of course, being slightly unfair. There are numerous well-known individuals working in the media who are, without doubt, proper geezers. Johnny Vaughan, host of *The Big Breakfast* on Channel 4, is probably the best example you will find, but Danny Baker and Chris Evans, love them or loathe them, can also be held up as fairly decent examples of geezerdom.

However, the fact remains that being laddy and constantly in the public eye does not give you the right to expect respect, nor to be thought of as a geezer. True geezers are people you know, admire and can trust. And that, in most cases, means either your family or your mates. With one obvious exception.

As the author of this book, and therefore your teacher, mentor, guide, call it what you will, I have to be regarded not only as a geezer, but as a better geezer than you. Read on.

Chapter Two

Why Football?

Bill Shankly once famously remarked that football wasn't a matter of life and death, it was more important than that. He was, of course, talking total bollocks, as any supporter with any kind of life will tell you. Nevertheless, he kind of had a point. Football is important, very important, and if you are ever to take your place amongst the élite world of the geezer, it is vital that you understand exactly what being a football fan is all about.

The first thing to realise is that being a supporter can be a frustrating, heartbreaking business and it is not something to be undertaken lightly. I am not too big to admit that I have stood on the terraces at Vicarage Road, or wherever, with tears streaming down my face as my beloved Hornets have been relegated (again), lost to the scum (again) or been beaten at Wembley (only once but that was enough, thanks). Yes, the Golden Boys have broken my heart more than once. Losing is an important part of football and, awful though it is, it is inevitable that you will go through it. Some more than others, admittedly, but you get the picture.

However, on the plus side, football can also be the most exhilarating thing you will ever experience. Getting to Wembley, beating the scum 4–0 at their place, winning the championship on the last day of the season – they're the things that make it all worth while. Days that you live off for months on end. The great beauty of football is that you never know which it will be as you walk through that turnstile, and that is why so many people do it. It's that feeling that this one may be *the* game. Someone once described the game as 89 minutes of boredom punctuated with one minute of elation or tragedy, depending on the result, and he was spot on.

The other thing you must understand is that watching Sky Sports or *Match of the Day* does not make you a football fan. It makes you a fan of football. There is a very important distinction there and it is one you should pay great heed to. It is, after all, a great weapon to use when arguing with people less important than yourself (i.e. women, anoraks and fans of other clubs) and one to which there is no credible response. The difference between the two is that as a football fan you don't care about how English clubs do in Europe or which striker will play up front for England, you only care about your own chosen team, nothing and no one else. Not only that, but you care enough about them to actually get off your fat arse and go and watch them in the flesh. This, in itself, gives you a degree of superiority over those who do not actually go to football.

This feeling is never stronger than when you find yourself in the company of those most hated of creatures, the 'armchair fans'. Yes, I fully understand that if you are a newcomer to football you may well actually have been an armchair, but from now on, forget that. I forgive you and you must never speak of it nor admit to it ever again. As a football fan and a geezer, you are to treat these people with utter contempt at all times. It is your duty. After all, they are responsible for many of the changes that have affected the way that people watch football in recent years. They may well sit there in their freshly ironed replica shirts, talk endlessly about the skills of Beckham or the marvel of Owen and think they're as good a supporter as you and me, but deep down they know the truth. They are inferior. Armchairs, after all, will watch whatever shit is broadcast to them. You actually go to football and, figuratively speaking, you make the noise they hear as they sit there with their dinner on their laps.

This air of superiority, once readily accepted as a good thing to adopt, will soon become one of the more important and invaluable traits you will have as a geezer. After all, you have (or should have) total faith in your own lads (even when they are crap) and you should be proud of yourself for following them. This means that as a follower of your chosen side your views are the most important in any discussion about them and any criticism, unfounded or not, is personal. It is, after all, directed at *your* lads, for God's sake! Not only that, but when you watch any other teams play (which will only be on telly, as you would never pay your hard-earned money to watch any game your lads weren't involved in) you will be able to watch them with an air of disdain peppered with torrents of abuse. They are, after all, inferior to your lads if for no other reason than *you* do not support them. It matters not one single jot that you follow Halifax or Brighton and that Man United are on the box (again). Similarly, when discussing the game with those who do not bother to go, you will be able to dismiss their views as totally irrelevant. After all, what do they know? Only what they saw on the box or read in the papers. That's second-hand opinion. If you were there, you will have seen it all first-hand, and if it was a game you weren't at because your lads weren't playing, then who cares?

Another important difference between football fans and fans of football is that for the armchairs football really is just about those 90 minutes. Forget all the other crap, the pundits, the adverts, etc. For them the game is 22 men running around chasing a piece of very expensive plastic. But for you, as a real football fan, it isn't like that at all. It is about much more.

Some would argue that football is about the battle between rich and poor and is representative of the class struggle still taking place in our society. Some believe it mirrors the time – if the game as a whole is crap then so is the country – whilst others believe that it represents good against evil (although, to be fair, Leeds United supporters' loathing of all things Lancastrian is taken much too far sometimes). But it is none of these. Yes, the game is full of passion, frustration and wonder, but the actual result, like the game itself, is, in the main, relatively unimportant. Some of the best days you will have as a supporter will be at games where your lads get dicked. That's the way it is. There is no rational thinking behind it and you should never try to apply any. Watching football is totally irrational, you must get to grips with that. It isn't about great players, Premier League football or even winning, for that matter. If it were we'd all support Arsenal or Man United, but we don't. There's more to it than that. Supporting a club that are crap can be the dog's bollocks (and, as a Watford fan, I should know) because you live in hope that it *can* get better. It has to. That's why Manchester City get such massive crowds. It's all down to good old blind faith and optimism. Believe me when I tell you that they will become your best mates. For most football supporters they'll have to, because you'll spend enough time in their company.

No, football isn't about great tactics, cup wins or even politics. It's about comradeship and about belonging. Sharing events and emotions with your mates and belonging to something that will come to dominate your weekends, if not your life. Welcome to the world that is football. God bless it!

Chapter Three

Choosing your Club

When you choose to make your way along the rocky road of football fandom, the first thing you must decide is not what club to support but how that choice came about. After all, as a newcomer to the world of the geezer you must realise that the very worst insult you can ever level at a footie fan is that he is a new-breed fan, an armchair or, even worse, a glory hunter. One only has to look at the problems Man United fans have to deal with to see that. The admission that you are a United fan brings immediate condemnation from supporters of almost every other club in the land, which in turn means that if you are a true United fan, as opposed to an armchair United fan, you have to justify your support.

As a geezer, you should be confident enough not to have to justify yourself or your support to anyone else, but it is inevitable that sooner or later you will be called upon to do so. Therefore, you need to get your story straight if you are to avoid immediate detection once you are amongst the die-hards. This story, once developed and firmly in place, must not only be cast-iron, it must 'prove' that you have supported your club all your life. Therefore it must, at all costs, avoid phrases like 'I used to watch Chelsea but left when they sacked Ruud'; 'I only started coming here because I've just moved to the area'; 'I was given free tickets', etc. All perfectly reasonable to the average fan, but to the die-hard geezer total anathema. And so, to enable you to construct a story so convincing that even your own mother would fall for it, we had better take a long look at some of the more traditional methods employed by supporters when choosing the love of their life, and then we will explore a few possibilities that may well appeal to you.

Before we do that, it is important that you remember that whatever team you choose to follow, be it Manchester United, Arsenal or Halifax Town, once that choice is made, there is no going back. If you're going to be both a true football fan and a geezer, it is essential that you make the right decision because you only get one go at it. It isn't like marriage, because you can divorce 'er indoors quite easily but changing clubs is totally unacceptable. Especially for geezers. Yes, of course there are people who do it, but there are names for them and they are, without exception, not very nice. Whatever you choose, be it Liverpool or Hartlepool, that name will be engraved on your heart for eternity. Players come and go, managers get the sack and clubs are sold, but the soul of the club and its name will become a part of you. Indeed, I would go so far as to say that the club, any club, *is* its supporters, and once you become one of them you are a part of it for ever. Even if your club goes bankrupt or simply falls out of the Football League altogether, then you have to accept that there will only be two options available to you: a lifetime of non-league footie or a change of sport. There is no other choice, and so it is vital that you get it right first time.

Clearly, fathers have a pivotal role to play here because for many supporters there will be no choice, as it will have been made for them long before they were born. I mean, what dad in his right mind would ever accept his son following another club? Of course, there are numerous examples of sons who rebel against their father's wishes and follow their old man's traditional rivals, but this should be avoided at all costs. Not only is it petty, it is risky. After all, in most cases the choice is narrowed down to just one other local club, and there is always the chance that your old man's team will be better than the one you are left with. This opens up the opportunity for him to take the piss out of you every time the two clubs meet, and do you really want a lifetime of that? Of course, there is always the chance that he supports the poorer of the local clubs and so, on the face of it, you end up with the better deal. But no, sadly this is far from being the case, because then he can always hit you with the accusation that you are a glory hunter. Face it, if your dad is a real footie fan, as opposed to an armchair, it's always better to follow in his footsteps if for no other reason than when you're skint he will always let you borrow money for your ticket.

If your old man isn't a fan then the chances are that the choice of which team to follow will come down to peer pressure or locality. If the school yard is full of Wolves fans it would take a brave, not to mention big, Black Country lad to avoid the lure of the pack and support the Baggies. Cowardice is, and always will be, a perfectly reasonable excuse for choosing a particular club. Similarly, others will simply follow their local side and I am proud to admit that I am one such individual. In fact, I have to say that I have little time for anyone who refuses to follow their local side unless they have a very good excuse — and 'because they're crap' is not acceptable unless you live in L*t*n.

There is another option, of course, but it is one to be avoided at all costs and is also the one that I personally find very unpalatable: television. The problem here is that choosing a team off the telly smacks of a past life of armchairdom, something you, as a geezer, can never admit to if you want to retain any credibility. You must remember at all times that, however you chose it, your love of your club has been lifelong. Telly equals the '90s equals successful equals clingon. Choosing to support a team just because they're winners, whilst clearly advantageous from a personal perspective, is not good enough. There is no loyalty nor honour to be gained from it, and should the truth come out, and it is inevitable that eventually it will, you will end up regarded as the very worst kind of fan even by those you have come to regard as mates. They will have put up with all the crap times, the defeats, the long journeys and the abuse and you won't. Your right to be regarded as one of them will cease immediately.

As a geezer, it is your duty to view television with disdain. We have already discussed armchairs and I need say no more on that, but, as a true fan, television should be despised because it is the sole reason why not all cup games are played on a Saturday, kick-off times move around like Alan Shearer's elbows and Gary Lineker is still in full-time employment. Television does, however, have one good use. If you're desperate for a reasonable excuse for falling in love with your side then the good old telly will provide it. But it is only acceptable if you can quote a pre-Sky game, because that will mark you out as someone who has passed puberty. The older the game, the better for you, and if you can quote the name of a particular player, all the better. It's all down to research. 'I fell in love with Peter Osgood after his diving header in the 1970 FA Cup final replay' is as good a line as you will ever hear. Especially if you manage to get tears in your eyes as you say it. Falling in love with Liverpool because you saw on *Soccer AM* that David James plays a lot of computer games hardly has the same impact. If you do decide to go down this route when choosing your team, get down the local library, drag out the video tapes of old games, study them and learn them off by heart. It's the only way.

Whilst the above are the more usual methods employed, it is fair to say that, over the seasons, teams have been chosen by supporters through a variety of odd ways: the first team on the teleprinter that day, sticking a pin in the pools coupon, following a team you once saw on holiday, etc. Laudable though these methods are, they should be avoided at all costs. There is something frighteningly sad about someone in Exeter following Peterborough United. Need I say more?

Of course, much of the information given above is relevant only if you already know which team you want to support. If you are one of those rare individuals who has discovered a love for the actual game of football rather than a love for a particular team, then I need to give you some guidance because this type of thing is totally inappropriate. The phrase 'I don't care who I watch as long as it's a good game' was invented for women and middle-aged men in flat caps. It is not to be used within earshot of real football fans and certainly not near proper geezers. You like football, you love your team. Understand that. This phrase must become so ingrained in your psyche that when you say 'I love football' you actually mean 'I love my club'. To the geezer, it's the same thing. The only time you can ever get away with anything other than this is if you decide to follow the national side rather than a club side. This is a very rare phenomenon and it should be discouraged, as generally it is used by groups of saddos to justify their desire to watch only those club sides who are doing well. If you meet any of these at any time they are to be ridiculed without mercy, because what they do is a cop-out.

So if your choice of club is undecided, I will give you a quick guide which may help point you in the right direction. But remember everything I have already told you before you decide, because, as I have said, you only get one shot at this. Once made, your choice can never be undone.

Distance is probably the most important factor to consider when you decide which team to follow, because whilst a long trip to an away game is one thing, a long trip to a home game is something else – primarily because it means less time drinking and socialising with other geezers. Fifty miles from your front door is probably the maximum I would consider. That should give you loads of scope, especially if you live in London. However, I would remind you that I am a firm believer in following your local league side and, no matter what standard of football they play, I would urge you to give them a go. They may already be a great side, but even if they're lower down the league, you never know, they may just get better and then you really can ride along on the crest of that particular wave. It's also worth remembering that even when they're crap, at least you won't have far to go home.

If you really do have to support a Premier League team and there isn't one on your doorstep, then a quick bit of research will tell you which ones have flirted with relegation in recent seasons. Once you have worked this out, these clubs should be avoided unless heartbreak and suicide are things you consider appealing. I would also stay away from teams who have won something the previous season as their fans will be on the lookout for glory hunters and will abuse anyone new. Personally, I would avoid the more obvious Premier League clubs because you will spend a lifetime justifying your support. As I have already mentioned, Man United suffer more than most from this with all that 'only City fans live in Manchester' rubbish, but Liverpool supporters also have to put up with it. These days, an accent like an extra from *Brookside* and a ready wit like Jimmy Tarbuck's are not obligatory if you want to watch your football from the Kop and so you will find people from all over Britain there. Conversely, supporting any of the teams from the north-east is a non-starter if you don't have a decent Geordie accent because they will automatically have you down as a glory-hunting southern shite. This reaction will be the same even if you come from Birmingham. Newcastle United have suffered more than most in recent years from an influx of new-breed supporters and the

Range Rover set, and they are resented with a passion by the true hard-core fans.

For those who live in and around London, the choice of Premier League clubs to support is remarkable. However, I would avoid Wimbledon, primarily because they are and always will be crap and everyone else will feel sorry for you. Arsenal are fine if you can live with all the celebrity supporters (Nick Hornby, Angus Deayton, Tom Watt, Stavros, etc.), while Chelsea will always be a good bet if you don't mind your club being run by a mad dictator who charges you a fortune to get in (unlike at Wimbledon where tickets are freely available and very cheap, a reflection of their previously mentioned quality and status). West Ham are an excellent choice, but if you want to follow the Hammers it is vital that you already have links with the East End as the fans of this club are passionate about both their area and sorting out interlopers. Watching the BBC version is not acceptable. Supporting Tottenham Hotspur should be avoided at all costs.

If you want to follow any of the other Premier League teams, I would urge you to listen to what I have told you about local clubs and consider them on a regional basis. Of the more attractive teams, Leeds United, Sheffield Wednesday and Barnsley are fine but only if you live in Yorkshire (and, let's face it, who else would want to go there?), whilst if you're a resident of the Midlands, Coventry and Aston Villa are always good bets for an interesting season, especially if you like hurling abuse (although in the case of these two clubs it is usually directed at your own players or the board). These two clubs have the added bonus of excellent motorway access should you decide to leave quickly, and judging by the traffic jams on the M6 most Saturday evenings, plenty do. Of the rest, Derby County are always worth a go if you like your football, not to mention your fellow supporters, simple, while Blackburn are worth considering if you want to follow a club whom no one else cares about. The rest should really be avoided unless you think you will be happy with a season of boredom and monotony peppered with the odd fleeting glimpse of decent football or you actually do live in Southampton.

Strange as it may seem, for the geezer, clubs outside the Premier League are often more attractive propositions because there is more chance of getting tickets and less chance that you will get elbowed out by either a greedy board or more affluent supporters. There is also the chance that you will be allowed to actually stand up during games and to be more abusive towards both players and other supporters. These are attractive features, the benefits of which should not be underestimated, and they are certainly things we will discuss later on. However, while the lower divisions do indeed provide more choice when selecting your club, it should also be remembered that, on the whole, the standard of football is far less appealing. Also, in the cold light of day, supporting York City hardly has the same status as following a club such as Leicester City. Then again, if you really have to, you can always watch Premier League football on the telly, as most of your games will still be played on a Saturday.

If you do opt to go for a Football League team, then, once again, region and distance should form the basis of your choice. However, there will always be some teams who are more attractive than others because they provide the opportunity to get on the bandwagon before it starts. Again research is important, because if a new manager has come in, the club has recently been sold or there is a strong youth-team policy, things could pick up quite quickly. The local papers provide an excellent source of research material and should be studied at great depth. Nothing is more appealing to football fans than the sweet smell of success.

To give you my thoughts on every league club would take far too long but what I will do is tell you which clubs should be avoided at all costs and why. However, at this point I must stress that whilst this information is based on years of knowledge, research and experience, I can only guide you. I accept no responsibility should you go against my advice and decide that watching the great game at Swindon Town might be a good idea.

Starting, as all good things do, from the south, Brighton should be avoided at all costs unless you like having a team shirt that looks like a Tesco carrier bag, love organising protests and have a caravan. Southend, whilst a great town, is a crap club. Indeed, most Saturdays see a mass exodus of football fans leaving the town and heading for Upton Park, which should tell you something. Why anyone would even consider pledging their support to Gillingham remains a mystery.

Within the bounds of the M25, Fulham, Brentford and Orient should be left well alone because nothing will ever happen at any of those clubs and if it does it will only be a tiny blip on a lifetime of tedium, and who would want that? Millwall, whilst probably the ultimate geezer club, must be left well alone, primarily because if you never saw a game at the original Den the supporters currently suffering at the New Den will eat you. Alive.

Out east, people who follow either Norwich or Ipswich usually do so because they have no choice, whilst out west avoid Reading (because they are doomed to fail) and Wycombe Wanderers (because they are, well, Wycombe). Any football fan looking for a club to support in Bristol should move. Immediately. Further west, in the beautiful land that is Wales, local loyalties dictate that football fans have no choice about which club they should support. That is unless they live in Wrexham, where, judging by the number of coaches that head north every Saturday, Liverpool seem to provide a decent, and certainly more attractive, alternative to the local lads.

North of London, Watford should be avoided for the simple reason that I go there and will spot you as a newcomer straight away (with obvious consequences), whilst you should never even go to L*t*n. And yes, that includes the town. After all, the people who live there are so desperate to get away themselves that they even build cars in a factory right next to the M1 to facilitate their own exit. Northampton are far too new to be taken seriously, whilst Notts County are just too bland.

In the footballing hotbed that is the Midlands, the first club to avoid are Walsall, as they have an appalling kit. Wolverhampton Wanderers are destined to a lifetime of doom and despondency and, on a personal note, should also be given a wide berth for their treatment of the great god Graham Taylor when he was their manager. Birmingham City, whilst a great club with great fans, have little or no credibility because they are run by a woman.

Up in the Potteries, Port Vale are the epitome of a boring and nothing club, whilst Stoke should also be left well alone for the simple reason that this is one club with more than its fair share of geezers already. The last thing it needs is any more. Further north, clearly the only reason anyone would want to support clubs such as Crewe, Tranmere, Huddersfield, Bradford, Wigan and Carlisle is that they actually live there and have no access to any kind of transport, whilst no one should support Oldham because I hate them. No, really, I do. Of course, the ultimate club not to swear your own undying allegiance to is Manchester City. Clearly a club destined to live in the shadows of a far more illustrious neighbour for ever. However, it is worth remembering that all football fans, no matter what their club, have the greatest of respect for City fans because of their plight, and so if you thrive on sympathy, not to mention hope, then City could provide a good bet. On the flip side, the blokes from Oasis 'support' them, which in itself is a good reason to give them a wide berth.

I must also say that, in my humble opinion, there is no justification whatsoever for any Englishman to follow a club which plays its football in Scotland, and that includes both Rangers and Celtic. Anyone who does this should be arrested and found guilty of treason, because not only are they letting down their country, it is also fair to say that Scottish football is crap. To be perfectly honest, everyone knows that anyway, and the only reason why the great Scottish public do not cross the border to watch English football instead of the poor product on offer to them is that they're too proud to admit that the English game is better. Scottish football has but one use and that is to fill up the pools coupons. Sorry and all that, but it's the truth.

While we're at it, I'd better make a brief mention about non-league football. Quite simply, don't. Leaving aside the obviously poor quality of football on offer, if you tell someone you support a non-league outfit, not only will they feel sorry for you but they will then patronise you, which is the very last thing you, as a geezer, would ever want. I'm not saying you wouldn't have a good laugh as a non-league fan but, let's be honest, when you get this far down you don't need to try and fit in because all those already there will be so glad to see a new face they'll welcome you like a long-lost cousin. I know it's harsh, but I do have to admit that one of my brothers is a passionate supporter of a non-league club and so I know it to be true. The obsession that is football is never sadder than when you're listening to someone talking passionately about a trip to Tilbury Town. And I refuse to even talk about women's football.

I should add at this point that although your choice of football club is for life, there is one light at the end of what, for many, is a very long and very dark tunnel. You see, once your primary choice is made, you are duty-bound to hate every other club and its supporters with a passion. But as this can cause immense depression should you support a club like Man City, it is vital that you allow yourself some degree of hope and a little ray of sunshine. For footie fans, that hope is provided by your second team. All fans have a soft spot for a second club; it is obligatory if for no other reason than it allows you to patronise someone else. However, unlike with the love of your life, you are allowed to change your second club occasionally. This gives you a degree of flexibility, allowing you to drop clubs who suddenly do something you don't like or who beat you in the cup. For example, I used to have a soft spot for Fulham until Kevin Keegan went there. As I do not like Mr Keegan, my goodwill towards them vanished. Now I keep a watchful eye on Barnsley, because I have a couple of good mates up there and I like the fact that the supporters have total belief in themselves and their team.

The other great benefit to this concept can be found as you travel home from watching your own lads get dicked. Because when the results are announced, you may well be able to say 'At least Barnsley won', which may, or may not, cheer you up a bit. Of course, Barnsley could have lost as well which means you'll be doubly pissed off, but that's the chance you have to take. Your choice can come from anywhere within the British leagues (or even beyond, but that's pointless really), and the beauty is that you do not have to justify it to anyone because everyone understands the logic of it already. For some reason Scottish clubs figure strongly in this concept, but I prefer to ignore north of the border altogether. At least as far as football goes.

Now that we have examined some of the more traditional methods utilised by supporters in choosing their teams and have discussed which team you should, or should not, follow, we can begin to plan out possible anecdotes for you to 'adopt' or modify to suit your own situation. However, you must remember, and I cannot stress it enough, that whatever tale you come up with, it must be credible and sustainable. After all, amongst the first questions to come your way when you appear on a terrace will be 'Who the fuck are you?', closely followed by 'Where have you been, then?'. You must be able to answer these in a manner that is so matter-of-fact it positively demands to be believed.

Earlier I talked at length about fathers and the role they have to play in all of this, but now I have to make a confession. My dad supports Spurs. Thankfully, this support lapsed in the early '60s when he moved out of London and so the fact that I do not follow his club is his fault. After all, he always refused to take his sons to White Hart Lane, and so eventually, after a brief dalliance with Chelsea – allowable as a teenage schoolboy and, in my defence, I did actually go – I rebelled and began to watch my local side, Watford. I will not replicate his mistake with my own son who, young though he is, has already gone through two replica shirts and has witnessed the Hornets in action on a number of occasions.

However, my example provides a good illustration of the way fathers can be employed as you plan out your own story. Whilst rebelling against your old man and supporting his arch rivals is never a good idea, rebelling and supporting another club is always worth considering because he can always provide a good excuse. For example, if you get on with your old man, then 'My dad moved here when I was younger but he was born in Manchester' is a classic and very valid excuse for following Manchester United. Similarly, 'My dad was born in Islington but has spent the last 20 years working with the Forces/Foreign Office/Secret Service and we've just come back to live in north London' provides a great justification for your sudden appearance at Highbury.

Conversely, if you hate your dad and the chances of him ever attending games with you is as remote as those of Paul Gascoigne winning *Mastermind*, then football provides the ideal opportunity to finally get something positive out of him. 'My dad's a complete twat and supports Spurs' may well be a statement of fact but it is hardly likely to excuse your sudden appearance amongst the hordes at Upton Park. Whereas 'My dad died last month and I promised him on his death-bed that I'd move from the stands to behind the goal where we scattered his ashes on Thursday' will gain you instant cult status.

If you fall in love with your local side, then 'You cheeky fucker, I only live down the road' spoken in a forceful manner will almost certainly work, but this leaves the problem of explaining your sudden appearance. An adaption of the 'I always watched from the stands with my dad but he died last month' line should work quite well here. It should also be noted that the introduction of a few expletives is always highly recommended.

If you have a problem using the good name of your father, then you need to come up with something a little more inventive if you are to blend in. 'I had to move from the stands, all those bloody women and kids were pissing me off no end' is always worth considering. However, there are things that should be avoided at all costs. For example, if you're old enough to drive, 'I've just moved here' will earn you instant abuse because it is totally unacceptable. After all, you can be almost anywhere within a few hours these days. Similarly, anything to do with women should be avoided like the plague. 'I always watched from the stands with my bird/wife/sister but I blew her out last month' might seem like a good idea at the time but it is courting disaster. No geezer worth his salt would ever take a woman to football. Remember that, because we will certainly talk about it later.

If you do make it into a ground and are ever faced with blokes who want to know who you are and why you've suddenly appeared in their midst but do not want to use one of the aforementioned excuses, the best approach to the situation is to bluff it out. If you have the nerve, 'Never mind me, mate, who the fuck are you?' may well get your inquisitor thinking that he has actually seen you before and he may come on to you like an old friend to avoid looking a twat himself. Be warned, though; if you take this approach, you have to be very careful who you're talking to. For example, 'What the fuck's it got to do with you?' may work extremely well when someone enquires as to your identity, but if he happens to be the top boy of the club's main mob, you will almost certainly be in extreme danger.

Another angle is to use the old 'I've been banned from all grounds for the last two years' ruse, or even 'I've just come out of prison', although if you use that one you do need to know the name of a prison and where it is. Chances are, someone within spitting distance may well have spent some of their past years residing at Her Majesty's pleasure and will know the score.

If, despite your bluffing, the other geezers continue to question your allegiance, you need to be sure of your facts before you carry on speaking. We haven't mentioned research much yet, but if you really do want to become a geezer it is vital. You need to know as much detail of the history of your chosen club as possible, but, and here's the trick, keep it to yourself and, for God's sake, don't blurt it all out. Telling everyone that you were at the Coventry game in 1982 and that the score was 0–0 and the referee was . . . etc., etc. merely marks you up as an anorak. Real geezers are confident enough with their allegiance to remember only the basics and not care about the rest.

Whilst we're on this subject, it is extremely important to realise that you must never pretend to have been somewhere you were not. Nothing blows your cover quicker than being found out and, believe me, eventually you will be found out. If someone asks you if you were at such-and-such a game, say you weren't and have a very good excuse ready to explain your absence. Someone died, your car broke down on the way, you were arrested outside the ground, anything. But never, ever say you were there if you weren't. Remember, if someone you don't know asks you where you were standing at Wembley during the 1983 cup final, it's because he's lining you up for a fall. Football fans are proud of their own track record and they don't like people ripping it off.

The key to all of this is to get your story straight, put together enough evidence to back it up and, if anyone asks, be ever so slightly arrogant when you respond. Once you have your story in place, rehearse it at length, practise it on tape and even film yourself on video if you can so that you can actually watch yourself and pick up anything that you get wrong. After a while you will actually begin to believe it yourself, and once you're at that stage you're ready to try it out for real. Believe me, it'll be worth all the trouble.

Chapter Four

What to Wear

Having decided which team will benefit from your patronage and constructed a story so convincing it would survive the scrutiny of an undercover journalist from the *News of the World*, it stands to reason that the next move will be to actually go to a game. Wrong. Walking through a turnstile is just a part of being a geezer and going to football. There are the small matters of apparel and socialising to be dealt with before we get to that stage.

The first thing we need to discuss is what you wear. One of the most important aspects of being a geezer is that every time you go to football you're showing out. It's a performance, not a pantomime, and you need to prepare yourself accordingly. You can be whatever you like during the working week, but come match day you have to slip on the uniform and persona of a geezer. After all, you'll be spending the day doing things that are totally alien to your everyday life.

You must be smart and comfortable, of course, but the key word is casual. Your dress is of paramount importance because it will, if you get it right, become your identity. However, before we get on to what you should wear, we'd better look at some of the things you shouldn't be seen dead in. A simple mistake will destroy your credibility at a stroke.

Strange as it may seem, replica shirts are a complete non-starter for geezers. Yes, I know that millions of them are sold every single season, but they are worn by kids, new-breeds and armchairs. A replica shirt means that you have fallen into the

34

commercial exploitation trap set up by your club to separate
you from your hard-earned money. This is unacceptable for a
geezer, who is, after all, aloof, arrogant and far too clever to fall
for such a scam. Not only that, but as a geezer everyone at your
club should damn well know what team you support, and if
they're opposing fans that air of mystery will keep them on
their toes. Of course, all supporters, even geezers, have replica
shirts, but all true geezers know that they should only be worn
at home, on holiday or when playing in the park with your
mates. And a little tip here: it is always better to have the away
strip, as this marks you out as a travelling fan. That is unless your
team's second strip was designed by someone suffering from a
drug-induced flashback or by someone clearly aged under
seven, in which case avoid it at all costs. It is also worth noting
that when you purchase your replica shirt, it should never, ever
have the name and number of a player on the back. You can
have cryptic messages such as 'We 8 L*t*n' or 'Watford 4 Ever'
put on it, but as it is unlikely you will ever come up with
anything original, better to leave it blank. Similarly, scarves are
to be avoided, as are any kind of flag or banner, as these merely
mark you out as a scarfer or an anorak. And if you even think
about wearing gloves . . .

Before we move on, a quick word about two other types of
replica shirt, neither of which will be mentioned again within
the pages of this book. If you are a football fan of, say, Bolton
Wanderers, there is no reason on this earth to justify the wearing
of an Ajax, Juventus or Brazil team shirt. If your own shirt isn't
good enough for you, you have no right to call yourself a true
supporter. Similarly, why on earth would anyone actually want to
own an England shirt? We all know that our clubs rip us off at
every opportunity and we accept that as the status quo, but to fall
for it with the national side beggars belief. As a geezer, you have
to be above all of this, and anyone who wears a shirt from any
team other than the one he supports deserves all the abuse you
are duty-bound to give him. And yes, that does include the
national side. Furthermore, anyone who actually has the brass
neck to walk into the ground where your boys play wearing any
kind of replica shirt other than that of either of the two teams on
the park deserves to be physically abused (not that I would
condone that, of course, but . . .). Oh yes, and by the way,

supporting Rangers or Celtic does not give you the right to wear your team shirt at every other ground in the entire world. It simply marks you down as a fuck-wit because you're not in Glasgow on a match day.

As with all rules, there is, of course, an exception, and that is if your lads get to Wembley. If this happens, you are obliged to wear your colours because whether it be the FA Cup final or the third division play-off, it will be one of the great occasions of your supporting life and for that reason you need to be in your shirt. It is, after all, one of the most important things you will ever own and, in any case, you need half that ground to be in your club colours.

Unless it is freezing, hats are another non-starter – with just one exception, and we will discuss that in a minute. The reason for this is that, generally speaking, they look ridiculous on geezers who are, after all, stylish individuals. Why spend a fortune on clothes and grooming and then stick something on your head? I mean, baseball caps and beanie hats are bad enough but whoever thought that wearing those jester-style aberrations to football was a good idea needs castrating.

Another reason for giving hats a miss is that they mess up your hair. Hair is very important to geezers, as it is the crowning glory and needs to show you have style. Geezers should have easily managed, neat, tidy and well-cut hair. When choosing a particular style, weather must always be taken into account, as it is highly likely that you will be at a game where it is pissing down and nothing looks worse than a wedgie haircut in a Manchester downpour. It is also worth remembering that anything which sets you apart from the norm has to be avoided, as it will allow others to take the piss. Northerners in particular have some very strange hairstyles, most of which seem to date from the '70s, and these, far from being stylish, simply provide a source of great merriment to those who live in the south. Any kind of facial hair should also be avoided as it always gives rise to the suspicion that you a: have something to hide, or b: are ugly. Oh yes, and only ponces have pony-tails and, despite the best efforts of Chris Evans and Mick Hucknall, ginger hair will never be fashionable on blokes.

If you're going bald, the only thing you can do is shave your head. Yes, I know it's drastic, but a hairstyle like a Sicilian monk or, for that matter, Clive Anderson is hardly in keeping with the image of a geezer. Radical though this course of action is, however, it does have a number of benefits, one of which is that you alone are allowed to wear a hat. After all, none of your mates would want you to catch hypothermia, nor, for that matter, sunstroke. Having a shaven dome also means that the police will inevitably think you're hard and so they will keep a very watchful eye on you. Something that may well come in very handy, should anyone decide to take exception to your presence. For some reason, you also get served faster in banks and post offices.

Finally, before we go on to discuss what you *should* wear, there is one more thing we need to talk about and it is a practice you should immediately learn to hate with a passion: face painting. There is something about the sight of a grown man with his face coloured in which, for me, is frighteningly sad. Quite why anyone over the age of eight thinks this is a good idea is beyond me but it is something that seems to be creeping into the British game more and more these days. Never, ever even think about it, and if anyone you know ever comes to a game painted in this way he should be ridiculed without mercy and then ostracised. However, I should add that, on the flip side of this, one of the greatest sights ever seen in football was the face-painted Scottish hordes traipsing away from Wembley after England had stuffed them during Euro '96. I never knew tears made face paint run like that. But other than that, face painting should be left to small children and Boy George.

And so, on to your clothes. The things that separate the true geezers from the rest. Someone once said that you either have or you haven't got style, but he was wrong because I am about to show you how to get it. You see, if you line 20 blokes up against a pub wall, the geezer will stand out a mile. He is the one that has style, and although the aim is always to blend in and not stand out, class shines through. Every time.

Terrace fashion is all about labels. Not bloody great triangles or silly ticks, but tiny little signatures or initials. Invisible to the anorak but blinding to other geezers. In the golden days of the casual scene it was all Ellesse, Lacoste, Tacchini, Fila and Diadora, but now these are old hat and the '90s geezer avoids them like the plague. The reason for this is that nowadays they are available everywhere and are reasonably cheap, which means they have lost their exclusivity. Similarly, the sports labels such as Adidas, Nike, Umbro, Reebok and Kappa should be avoided because the main market for these clothes now seems to be spotty teenage girls out shopping. Hardly the stuff of the terraces. And while we're on the subject of sports labels, anything that has a massive logo on the back merely marks you out as a dickhead, which is another reason why Puma, O'Neill and Penn also fail to make the grade. It is also important to remember that any label that has fallen victim to the forgers should be avoided. After all, you may well have paid 60 notes for that Ralph Lauren shirt but the bloke next to you may have got his for a fiver at a dodgy boot market and it will look just as good as yours after a three-hour train journey. It's a tragedy, I know, because the genuine stuff is real class, but you, as a geezer, can't take the risk that someone might possibly question the quality of your clothes. For this reason alone, the following labels should be avoided:

Tommy Hilfiger
Yves Saint Laurent
Ralph Lauren
Hugo Boss
Helly Hansen
Calvin Klein

No, if you're talking labels, you're talking the following:

Kent and Curwen
Burberry
Duffer of St George
Ted Baker
Henri Lloyd
Paul Smith
SixEightSevenSix
Versace
Dolce and Gabbana
Armani
Helmut Lang

Additionally, if you fancy being very pro-English, you could always try Dr Marten's range of clothes. They're the bollocks.

The other label universally accepted by all geezers (especially amongst those clubs from outside London) and the one single label that seems to have taken over as the uniform of the casuals in recent years is Stone Island. Indeed, if you have any doubts about the credibility of a particular label, leave it alone and find your nearest Stone Island stockist. You can't go wrong.

The average geezer, if there is such a thing, will be decked out in a combination of the following: Dr Marten shoes or Timberland desert boots; Levi 501s, Lois, Pepe or even Dr Marten jeans; a shirt (either T-, polo or long-sleeved) made by any of the above designers; and, if it's cold, a plain jumper by Henri Lloyd or Stone Island. Colours are always an area of great concern, but as a general rule pastel shades are best of all. Anything bright or garish will make you an easy target for abuse and/or the attentions of the Old Bill who will already be miffed that you are better dressed than they are. Avoid pink (obviously) and never wear a colour being worn by the opposing team. Similarly, the days of diamond jumpers and lairy jackets are long gone and there is a reason for that as well. I mean, who wants to look like Ronnie Corbett or Jimmy Tarbuck on a bad day?

This is all topped off with the geezer's ultimate accessory, the golf jacket. This is the most important item of all, and not just because it's the one on the outside. Other geezers will know who made your jacket before the badge, if there is a badge, becomes visible. They will do this by the style and cut of the said jacket, and it will immediately mark out the type of geezer you are and even, in some cases, what club you support. It is vital that you get this garment right. The best way to do this is to pay a few visits to your chosen ground and observe the geezers in their natural habitat. See how they act and what they wear and then go out and get the same. It won't fail. However, we all know people who would still look like a sack of spuds even if they were wearing an Armani suit, and so to avoid being one of these you need to take your time. Visit loads of shops and ask for help but, above all, look in the mirror and don't scrimp on the cash. Follow these golden rules and you're almost there. Remember, real geezers are confident enough to wear their labels on the inside.

If you have been paying attention, you should have noticed that so far I have made only a passing reference to the weather. There is a simple reason for this. For the geezer, the temperature on a match day is almost irrelevant. There is no logical reasoning to this and you should not try to find any. After all, in a country where football is watched in all types of weather, you would think that, out of all football fans, the geezers would have it sussed. But no. Devoting your life to geezerdom means that in the winter you will freeze your nuts off. That's just the way it is. Being immune to freezing cold temperatures or driving rain has become almost as much a part of being a geezer as being able to enjoy lager, and it is the same at almost every club in the land. Watch *Match of the Day* in the depths of winter and I guarantee that behind the goals will be hordes of geezers wearing only the obligatory golf jacket as protection against driving rain or freezing cold sleet. With one exception. The Geordies.

All football fans know that, when it comes to the climate, Geordies are mad. Pure and simple. The rain can resemble stair-rods or the snow can make watching the game akin to having interference on your telly, but the Geordie geezers will still be there in their T-shirts or, if the temperature is above freezing, even topless. I will never understand it and you should never try to copy it. Not unless you want hypothermia.

On those rare days when the sun shines, however, the geezers will occasionally leave their golf jackets at home and may even resort to wearing only piquet or polo shirts. Again, if this is the case, then great care should be taken when purchasing these garments. Stick with the labels you've seen on the other geezers and you won't go far wrong. Finally, geezers never, ever wear shorts at football. There are a number of reasons for this but the most important is that showing your legs invites piss-taking from other geezers, and who wants that?

So there you are, kitted out in wall-to-wall designer labels and looking the dog's bollocks. The next thing to do is to enjoy the match-day experience, but before we walk into the ground we should discuss a few more of the dos and don'ts.

Part Two
Match Days

Chapter Five

Down the Pub

Match day is, for most football fans and for all geezers, the most important day of the week. Every second is enjoyed, absorbed and digested and every act is a part of an experience most football fans grow up with. You are walking into that and so you need to know what goes on, because if you do anything at all out of the ordinary you'll stand out like a Spurs fan at an Arsenal Supporters Club Christmas party. From the moment you wake up, you must adopt the persona of a geezer and forget everything else in your life. Work, wife, debt, problems, everything. Today is football day.

On match days (and we'll refer to them as Saturdays, as I'm a sucker for the old traditional stuff) all football fans read either *The Sun*, *The Star* or *The Sport*. There is nothing to stop you reading either *The Times* or *The Express* as well, but at least one of the down-market tabloids is obligatory reading. The reason for this is that not only will everyone else have read them (which gives you something to talk about), but as you are going to spend the day in a testosterone-drenched environment, a good dose of tits and football is a fairly good way to start. Just as importantly, you should have a large cooked breakfast with plenty of hot, sweet tea. This is a must. Not only because eggs and bacon are what real men eat for breakfast but also because you will need food to keep you going through the day.

When you eventually walk out of the house, dressed in your finest, the papers should be taken with you and stuck in your back pocket so that you've got something to read later on. You should also take at least one packet of cigarettes with you. The reason for this is that while smoking may not be the healthiest act in the world, for you it will prove invaluable because those fags will serve a vital function as the day progresses. You see, as a geezer, one of the most important features of Saturday is the pre-match pint. It's where all the geezers gather and all the gossip and banter takes place, and if you're ever going to fit in, that's where you need to be. But you knew that, of course, and you will already know which pub because you will have researched that during the previous week (and if you're really clever you will also have found out the barmaid's name).

However, to return to the subject of smoking for a moment, the beauty of the old cancer sticks is that they not only settle the nerves, they also give you something to do. And not only that, but at some time during the day another of the geezers may well come up and ask you for a light or a fag. If they do that, you may well be able to engage them in conversation – which is, after all, one of the main aims. Oh yes, the brand of those fags should be Benson and Hedges, Embassy or Marlboro', because they are men's fags. Turn up with something menthol or French and you'll be hammered. And no geezer has ever smoked a pipe.

And while we're on the subject of brands, when you drink, it has to be beer or lager. Because real geezers drink beer or lager. No bitter lemon, white wine or even Bacardi and coke, just beer. Bottles are best and Budweiser or Becks are best of all, but if not, a simple pint will do. Soft drinks are only acceptable if you're on an away trip and you're driving or if you have a sexually transmitted disease and everyone already knows about it.

Now, initially, as you stand outside the local tavern, you will, not to put too fine a point on it, be shitting yourself. This is perfectly understandable, as it is, after all, a case of walking into the lions' den (literally, if you're in south-east London) and it is certainly the biggest test of nerve you will ever face. But if you are to graduate to the world of the geezer, you simply have to go in there, and if you do it like this you will have no problem.

If the pub has a bouncer on the door, something that seems to be on the increase these days, then merely saying hello to him should get you through the door (people being nice to bouncers is hardly the norm and they will not know how to react). If they question your allegiance, telling them your address or giving them the barmaid's name should do the trick. Once you're through the door, ignore all of the eyes that will immediately fall upon you and walk directly to the bar. Force your way to the front and shout your order at the barmaid. You should never, ever offer to buy anyone else a drink. This is totally against the principles of football fans who, having been fleeced for years by their clubs, prefer to spend what little they have left on themselves, although on away trips this rule is occasionally relaxed. Similarly, you should never ponce off others as this will lead to long-term resentment and possibly violence if you fail to pay back the debt. Once the barmaid has acknowledged your existence and taken your order, take out your paper, open it at the sports pages and light a fag. If she fails to hear you, keep shouting and waving your money. Keep looking directly at her and never make eye contact with anyone else. Football fans can smell fear a mile off.

Once your drink arrives, stand at the bar, drink half your pint and return to your paper and your fag. At this point, one of two things will happen. As you have stormed straight into the pub and shouted at the barmaid (using her name if you've been clever), everyone will assume you have been there before, and as you have a local accent they will also assume that you are a native. The pub will immediately return to normal and, hey-presto, you're in.

Alternatively, the pub will fall silent and someone will walk up and, using any number of variations, ask you who you are and what you think you are doing in their pub. At this point, you need to utilise the story developed earlier and after delivering it with confidence bordering on arrogance return to your paper, pint and fag. (You could also add 'I used to drink at the Rose and Crown but they're all wankers in there/I had a row with the barman and got banned/the beer is shit' which will also explain your appearance in the pub.) If it works as it should, your inquisitor will leave and you can get on with your drink in the sure-fire knowledge that they've accepted you. If not, er ... well, it might be best not to think about that. Well, all right, if things don't go as you planned and it is clear that the finger of suspicion is pointing firmly at you, you have a decision to make and you need to make it rapidly. You can either get out of there (and if you choose this option my advice would be to do it as quickly as possible) or you can stay and brave it out. If you take this option, inevitably someone will come up and start quizzing you at length about anything to do with the club. As we have already discussed, your research will have given you all the ammunition you need, but, remember, these geezers know their stuff and they will be looking for anything to trip you up. The key is to remain confident and to front up anyone who doubts you by adopting an air of total indignation. How could anyone have the nerve to question your allegiance? This will inevitably throw them off the scent and at this point they will either leave you alone or merely threaten to slap you one. If this looks likely, it is time to use the secret weapon. The enamel badge.

It is always worth wearing an enamel badge inside your golf jacket because it will almost certainly get you out of situations such as these. Showing someone that you wear the emblem of your chosen club is as good as naming the cup-winning side of 1927, but it cannot be any old badge. After all, anyone can walk into the club shop and buy the latest version. It must be an old badge, and the older the better. Scour boot markets or pester old relatives to find a suitable model and never go to a game without it. Remember how soldiers in the trenches used to carry Bibles in their breast pockets to protect their hearts and save their lives? This is the same thing, and it rarely fails. Once your inquisitor sees your badge, he will back down, apologise and may even offer to buy you a pint. If he does, this offer should never be accepted. Not only does he not really mean it, but taking beer off him will inevitably mark you down as a git. Better to merely tell him to forget it and return to your drink. He will immediately mark you down as a top bloke and will remember your face for ever because not only will you have walked into a pub full of geezers, you will also have stood up to one and shown a fair degree of bottle. Everyone there will remember you. Your path towards acceptance is almost complete.

Having made it through the opening exchanges, the pre-match pub can be a very rewarding place to be. However, integration remains the key and, to this end, you will eventually need to engage others in conversation. Well, that isn't strictly true, because you need to make sure others engage you in conversation. The best way to achieve this is to remain slightly aloof, passing comment only with those who barge you out of the way to get to the bar or, if you're lucky, those who are next to you at the bar. In the early stages, it is always best to remain at the bar for fear of sitting at the wrong table (geezers often have their own particular tables just as old gits do in dodgy old back-street pubs and, in any case, why upset the status quo?). Once someone actually strikes up a conversation with you, the team will obviously be the most likely topic for discussion and you should ensure that you are up to date with the latest developments to avoid any suspicion. Teletext or the local papers should provide all the information you will need.

A word of warning here: never say anything controversial about your own club for obvious reasons and never talk about any other team. Do that and you may as well write 'new bloke' in big red letters on your forehead. You are there to watch your lads, and that's all you should be thinking about. It may be that someone will start talking about other games or, more specifically, trips to other games, and if this happens, avoid taking part and remember the golden rule: never pretend to have been somewhere you were not. Someone will always find you out. If anyone asks you outright why you were not at a particular game, use of the old 'I was out of the country/in the army/in prison' excuse is highly recommended.

After a while, as you listen to others talking, you will begin to notice a strange phenomenon. You will begin to believe that you are experiencing recurrent *déjà vu*. This is not the case at all and you should rest easy. It is merely the fact that people are repeating the same stories over and over again. The reason for this is that football fans thrive on memories of good times and the pre-match pub is one of the few places where people can relate their personal experiences over and over again, and so, inevitably, they do. It's expected and made all the more strange by the fact that most of the people listening will not only have heard it a thousand times before but will actually have been there as well. Stay out of this for now and eventually, after a few years, you can tell of trips you *were* actually on.

If anyone starts talking about any other subject, it is always wise to stay out of these conversations as well, at least until you are more familiar with the individuals concerned. After all, everyone else in the pub may know full well that the bloke you are talking to was Margaret Thatcher's greatest fan and so calling her an old slapper will hardly endear you to him, will it? Aside from politics, religion is another topic to be avoided (primarily because you will spend much of the remaining afternoon screaming for divine intervention or a thunderbolt aimed directly at the man in black), as is anything to do with personal problems (after all, everyone has their own, so who wants to hear about yours?) or work (that's why you go to football, to forget that!). Similarly, mention either art, new man, your feminine side or the Internet and the other geezers will look at you as if you are mad. The subject of David Mellor is also best avoided unless you are insulting him.

Furthermore, never talk about sex until you are certain that you know everything about everyone else. You could drop yourself into all kinds of trouble. If others start talking about it, it will inevitably involve a tale of sexual prowess, group sex and/or perversions which will be so ludicrous (and clearly fiction) it will be funny, and so these are always worth listening to. Strangely, even in these enlightened times, you will never hear anyone talk about male homosexuality at football unless it is referring to rumours about the sexual leanings of a particular player. Lesbianism is, however, a frequent topic for discussion, although for some reason it is usually at the same time as group sex or fantasies. If you do get dragged into conversations of a sexual nature, never, ever admit to anything remotely iffy. That is where nicknames come from, and who wants to be known as Swarfega Man for ever?

Crime is another subject you will frequently hear about in pre-match pubs and you will quickly form the impression that all your fellow fans are villains. This is not true (unless you're a scouser) but is merely male chest-beating. If you can manage it, it is always worth having people think that you are slightly dishonest, but any claims need to be realistic and credible. Having a mate who can get hold of vanloads of dodgy electrical gear has a great deal more status in pre-match pubs than telling everyone you can get them as many paper-clips as they will ever need.

The bottom line is tread carefully and bide your time. Remember, as a rule the pre-match pub experience only takes place every two weeks, and so after you've done it a few times and people begin to recognise you you'll quickly feel like an old hand. In any case, as kick-off time approaches, everyone will leave. And so should you, because you have a game to go to.

Chapter Six

Outside the Ground

Depending on the distance between pub and ground (at Watford it's something like 30 feet), the sanctuary of the tavern should be left as late as possible to avoid sitting for ages inside the ground. Having avoided the consumption of huge amounts of alcohol, you should still be in a fit state to walk in a straight line, and as you stroll up the road you will see a number of things you would not normally see elsewhere. These include programme sellers, fanzine sellers, street vendors (selling scarves, badges, etc.) and hot-dog sellers. All of these are to be avoided at all costs, primarily to protect the contents of your wallet as well as, in the case of the hot dogs, your stomach. And here's why:

Programmes: These 'magazines' are put together by the commercial department of your club and are usually glossy, brightly coloured affairs designed to appeal to 'supporters'. To you, the geezer, this means two things. Firstly, despite the fact that they cost a fortune, they are full of adverts. Indeed, it is often thought that the wages of at least two first-team players at Watford are fully covered by the advertisers in our programmes. Secondly, and more importantly, they are full of propaganda. Inside the front cover will be a photograph of the manager alongside a message from him explaining how and why everything has gone wrong and how it isn't his fault, or how everything has gone wrong and it's the chairman's or the fans' fault. Flick over a few pages and you'll find an article about one of your own players and, further on, an article about the visiting

team (and who cares?). Towards the back lie the current tables –
which are always out of date due to the games played in
midweek – and the fixtures for the coming season, which are
usually depressing. After all, it's bad enough being in the second
division in the first place, but do you really need reminding that
you've got to go to Wigan in February? Programmes are to be
avoided as they simply mark you out as being a bit sad for falling
into yet another commercial trap. Not only that, but if you do
buy one, you'll spend the entire game trying to get it back off
everyone who has borrowed it off you.

Fanzines: These are comics put together by genuine fans in the
comfort of their own bedrooms with help from their friends on
the Internet. Most of them have 'comedy' names such as *I Can
Drive a Tractor* (Norwich), *Hoof the Ball Up* (Wimbledon) or *Brian
Moore's Head* (Gillingham) and most of them are crap. Content
ranges from how bad the current crop of strikers is to what a
great game the 1873 local derby was and the articles are only
really of interest to the people who wrote them. Originally, the
fanzines were designed to give fans the opportunity to vent their
anger at the club, but, sadly, this is rare now. Some fanzines are
simply page after page of vitriol aimed at local rivals, and these at
least are worth reading. However, generally speaking, if you feel
the need to read one, borrow it.

Street vendors: People who sell things in the street should be
arrested. Immediately. It is bad enough that they hawk their tat
outside your ground but they always have the brass neck to sell
the visitors' gear as well. This in itself is criminal. However, worse
than that, these people (who again always seem to come from
Manchester or Merseyside) always seem to have scarves, flags or
badges from all of the Premiership clubs. This is an outrage. I
would never advocate violence but . . .

Catering: The food sold at football matches, despite the best
efforts of the Premier League and Delia Smith, is woeful. Whilst
the stuff inside grounds is one thing (later), the stuff on sale
outside is frightening. Leaving aside the fact that the person
serving is almost certainly opposed to any kind of personal
hygiene, the food itself will inevitably be overpriced and, also

inevitably, overcooked. After all, that ten-inch sausage may have been sitting on that griddle for hours, and as for the onions . . . Well, you just know that most of them remain from the last home game. The hamburgers, or, as they are more affectionately known, dogburgers, are no better. Why do you think they stick cheese, relish and anything else on them if they can? Yes, I know they smell delicious, but that smell disguises all sorts of horrible things. Not least of which is a total absence of any kind of taste, and unless you think that vomit and diarrhoea would make attractive additions to your bathroom, steer well clear. If you must eat, chip shops or newsagents are the best bet. If not, hit the local burger bar. Forget mad-cow disease; how do you think Birmingham City fans got like that in the first place?

Two other groups you will come across and will inevitably make contact with at some point are policemen and stewards. These are the sworn enemies of the geezer and so before we go any further we should have a look at them.

Outside the actual ground (and we will look at their role inside stadia later on) stewards are there to advise you on which gate to enter and to give you advice on anything to do with safety or facilities. On the face of it a good idea, you would think. However, for some inexplicable reason, as soon as stewards pull on their luminous jackets they adopt the personality of a crazed dictator or the worst kind of jobsworth. This means that far from being consumed with a desire to satisfy the needs of their customers as they should be, they inevitably set out to upset as many people as possible, thereby spoiling their (and possibly *your*) enjoyment of the game. Therefore stewards are, almost without exception, to be regarded as complete and utter twats. After all, with the possible exception of Tottenham and L*t*n T*wn fans, what sane person would want to spend the entire game staring away from the pitch? It makes no sense. As a geezer, it is your duty to argue with stewards and to make their life a misery in the sure-fire knowledge that as long as you're not too abusive there is nothing they can do about it.

Similarly, outside grounds the role of the policeman is usually restricted to traffic control and keeping an eye on the activities of the geezers. As you will undoubtedly come under the watchful gaze of the Old Bill at some time or another, all policemen are to be regarded as bastards even if one of them happens to be your dad (and if this is the case, never, ever tell anyone about it). Like stewards, they too should always be argued with at every opportunity, primarily because arguing with a policeman will endear you to all of the other geezers in the immediate vicinity. There is, of course, always the risk that he will arrest you, but this is a risk well worth taking as most policemen are loath to do anything that would make them miss the game. Indeed, there is an art to arguing with policemen and knowing exactly when to back down to avoid arrest, but this takes years to master. As a rough guide, though, if he utters the phrase 'If you don't fuck off soon . . .' and starts foaming at the mouth, that's a good time to back off a bit. Inside grounds, however, policemen are an entirely different animal and we will discuss them a little later.

Before we move on, a quick word on the subject of horses. Policemen on horseback should always be given a wide berth. They shit and piss all over the ground, bite you and often tread on your toes as they push you around. The horses are slightly better trained but should still be avoided.

Another group of people you may well encounter as you walk towards the ground are individuals known to all and sundry as touts. In the good old days touts used to be easily identified by their gold bracelets and sheepskin coats, but these days spotting them is more difficult. However, if you see someone walking around apparently talking to himself in a thick Manchester accent, chances are he's a tout. Strangely, he will be asking if anyone passing by him has any tickets to sell when what he actually means is that he has, and he wants to sell them. Touts are to be regarded as a good thing. If a game is sold out, touts will always have tickets to sell, and although they might be slightly overpriced, it's all down to supply and demand. Strangely, given that previous Conservative governments were amongst the strongest advocates of free enterprise, neither the police nor the authorities agree with this practice and they have made touting illegal. This should not, however, deter you from dealing with them should your team ever be in the cup final and you have as much chance of getting a ticket as you have of actually playing in the game.

The final group you may well come across on your way to the ground are the opposing fans. For the geezers, this is where it gets interesting, and so you really need to know about them. Whilst we're at it, we'll take a look at the other types of fans as well.

Chapter Seven

Other Fans

As someone who aspires to be a member of that exalted breed the geezer, you should already have formed the opinion that every other football fan who walks into your home ground is inferior to you. This is perfectly true. A club, any club, is dependent on its geezers because the soul of the club lies in their hands. That is why they are so important. It is geezers who shout, scream and hurl abuse at all and sundry and therefore it is geezers who create atmosphere. Always remember that, because it – and by association you – is vital to the success of the game. However, loath as I am to admit it, football is watched by others apart from geezers and this is one subject we haven't really addressed yet. Although as a geezer you should treat all other supporters with disdain at all times, it is only right that I explain a little bit about these other interlopers so that you have something to focus on as you sneer at them.

One of the things about football fans in general is that they all think that they're the same. But they are not. This is a myth put about by people who wish that they were the same as the geezers. There are, in fact, a number of distinctive types of supporter, and although they all have a role to play, they are all very different indeed.

We have already looked at the subject of armchairs and I trust that you now understand that they are the lowest of the low, but only slightly up the evolutionary ladder are the people who inhabit executive boxes. These are the things that look like portakabins bolted to the back of the main stands and they are designed to enable people to watch the game from behind plate-glass. They are also a by-product of the drive towards commercialism that is destroying football as we know it. Invariably the people who inhabit these boxes will have got in for free and will not only have had a free lunch but will also be able to drink beer while watching the game. They will also quickly develop the habit of looking down their noses at anyone not fortunate enough to be sitting with them, and that means you and me. As a geezer, you simply cannot allow this, and so executive boxes are to be targeted for abuse at all times.

One step up from the armchairs and the corporate freebies are the anoraks or scarfers. These are people who always seem to find their way into the seats surrounding you and they are a pain in the arse. They are also the ones who buy the replica shirts and actually wear them at games and they are the ones who discuss tactics and make apologies for certain players who, according to them, are having a bit of an off-day. They sit there reading their programmes (which they carefully handle to avoid damage) and devour every bit of information given them, and they love it. If you ever hear anyone talking about statistics, fantasy football teams or programme collections, he's an anorak.

Another thing anoraks do is to carry radios to football. Quite why they do this has never been understood. After all, why listen to the results of other games when the most important team in your life is playing in front of your very eyes? Nothing can be more important than that. Amongst this group are also to be found the wannabes. That is, wannabe geezers. They are blokes without any kind of class or style and should be looked down upon at all times. Although they are one of the more vocal elements inside grounds, they also live in their replica shirts, read fanzines, talk to their 'mates' on the Internet late at night and are the one group responsible for the introduction of drums to football stadia. For this alone they have to be hated.

The next group we will find amongst supporters is the old gits. These people, as the title suggests, are old, and they are gits. They are the blokes who sit in the pubs moaning about the current team and how they will never be as good as the 1958 relegation side and how you used to be able to get into the ground, have a pint with the centre forward, buy two bags of chips (which were much bigger and better in those days) and still

have change from a shilling. Just think of your dad and you'll get
the picture. Avoid these men at all costs because their age hides a
great danger. After an hour in the company of an old git, he will
engage you in conversation and you will unavoidably find
yourself nodding as he speaks. Once this happens, unless you are
very careful, you will soon find yourself being sucked into his sad
little world and your day will be ruined.

After the old gits come the young gits, the kids. It is a fact that
kids will eventually grow into adults and from within their
number will inevitably come the next generation of geezers. For
this reason alone, kids are an abhorrence. After all, in the scheme
of things, one of them will end up taking over from you.
However, they are the future, and as long as they're over ten, have
a bit of respect for their betters and steer well clear of you, they
are at least bearable. Unlike any children under ten who should
be kept well away from football at all costs because they run
about and annoy everyone else.

Following on from the old gits and the young gits are the sads.
They are called that because many of them will be former
geezers who are now dads and are unable to enjoy the game in
the same way that you, as a young, virile bloke, can. Although
they should not be pitied, you should feel slightly sorry for them.
After all, there is no sadder sight than a geezer who has hit 35
sitting in a ground with his seven-year-old son.

Finally, we come across the lads. These are basically everyone
else between the ages of 15 and 30 who, although almost as
passionate and certainly as vocal as geezers, watch their football
bedecked in Adidas, Ellesse and Umbro clothes rather than
Duffer, Timberland or Stone Island. But, more importantly, they
have yet to realise that they, as supporters, are more important to
the club than the actual players. All geezers should realise that the
lads are the foot-soldiers of football fandom and therefore should
be grudgingly respected and certainly acknowledged.

Up to this point I have broken down the support into a
number of specific types, but there is one group that has yet to
be mentioned and that is women. And there is a reason for that.
I have said it before, and I will say it again: women and football
do not mix. As a geezer, you will spend your day in the company
of other men, and therefore women who go to football are to be
totally and utterly ignored. Furthermore, if you are unfortunate

enough to find yourself sitting near a woman, you should never, ever moderate your language. In fact, it is your duty to become even more colourful as she may well move, which would be a bonus. To be perfectly honest, if I had my way women wouldn't even be allowed inside grounds, and I certainly believe that if a ground is sold out and a male of the species is locked outside, someone should go in, grab the nearest female and throw her out so that the bloke can have her seat.

I have to say at this point that I get into a lot of trouble for my views on women at football, but I'm afraid that's too bad. I have yet to be told by any football-loving male that my opinions are contrary to theirs and that is good enough for me. And, let's face it, being a geezer is about being a bloke and doing blokey things. That's one of the attractions. Women who watch football will, of course, argue this point until the cows come home. They will argue that they love the game as much as me, go to every game home and away and can discuss tactics with anyone who cares to listen. Unfortunately by this time I am not listening, as I simply do not care about anything a woman has to say on the subject of my obsession. However, at some point or another during your life of geezerdom you will have to defend this stance, and so I will explain the reasoning behind it once again.

Generally speaking, men live for their football. They sleep it, worship it and, if they can, they play it. When they watch the game, they go through every emotion known, but in the background there is always an element of frustration. This frustration is borne out of the fact that if they had practised harder as a kid, they could have been out there doing it while some other sad git watched them. Women cannot do that because they can never play football and that is the difference. Men love football; women like football. It really is that simple. If ever you get into an argument with a woman about football, you do not need to sink to the level of 'you only go to look at the players' legs', but merely ask her to explain how she can possibly talk about Gascoigne failing to put that 40-yard pass on to the feet of Shearer when she could not kick a ball with any degree of accuracy over a distance of 40 inches. That will shut her right up. Alternatively, if a woman begins talking football with you, merely look at her and say, 'Yeah, right-oh, love,' before returning to your paper and you will be unbeatable.

In any case, there are only two reasons why most women go to watch football. For the married ones it's the only chance they get to spend time with their old man, whereas the single ones only go because they can spend a few hours surrounded by men in a testosterone-fuelled frenzy. This is clearly the case, because most single females who go to football are pig ugly.

A brief mention here about women's football. Football is, and always will be, a man's game. It is played by men for the enjoyment of other men and it is hard and aggressive, fast and skilful. All things that women's football isn't. The argument that women's football is all about grace and skill is a joke. I mean, have you ever seen any women footballers? Having studied the subject at great length, it is clear to me that women who try to play football fall into three categories: they are raving feminists and play the game because, if men do it, then they should have the right to, or they are geezer-birds. And by that I mean women who really want to be men (if they were under 11 we would call them tomboys). Or they are lesbians. Women's football is crap. If it were any good people would go and watch it, but it isn't and they don't. And, to be honest, I doubt they ever will.

Now, having looked at the various types of supporter, I need to point something out. All of the descriptions you have read refer to fans of your own team. Opposing fans are something else entirely. When you mention visiting supporters, there is no 'type'; they are all to be referred to as scum. Without exception. The reason for this is that they have come into your town with the express intention of entering the ground you worship and will, as a result, pollute it with their very presence. Not only that, but the fact that they haven't had the foresight to follow the same team as you means they are clearly lacking in mental capacity. As a geezer, you must treat all opposing fans with the utmost contempt. However, amongst their number will be groups of other geezers and these are to be treated warily. After all, they will also have the style and class you have. Not as much, obviously, but a fair bit, and so as much as you dislike them, you should have some degree of respect for them. You should also, however, treat them with caution. They are, after all, a dangerous breed.

Chapter Eight

Getting in and to your Seat

So there you are, walking up the road towards the ground. Warily keeping an eye on the opposing fans and the police. After weeks of research and hard work, the time is rapidly approaching when you will walk through that turnstile into what will become your spiritual home. Not only that, but if you have followed all my advice so far then you will be ready to take your place amongst the geezers. The group you have aspired to. But take care. You're not there yet, and having sorted out your clothes, survived the pre-match pub and had an·argument with a policeman, now is not the time to make a mistake.

The way in which you actually enter a ground is just as important as any other aspect of geezerdom. I mean, walking up to a steward and asking him where the big boys stand is hardly likely to win you any brownie points, is it? Again, any research you will have done will pay untold dividends here because you need to know in advance which part of the ground the geezers sit in and which turnstile to use to gain entry to it. There is no fixed rule here. At some clubs, the geezers sit behind the goal; at others, they sit at the side of the pitch. However, in all cases they sit low down. Never in an upper tier, as this would mean they couldn't abuse the players and/or officials at close range.

Furthermore, having worked out which turnstile to enter, you should be familiar with the layout of the ground and know exactly whereabouts in that particular section you intend to sit. This will avoid any embarrassing episodes. After all, appearing next to the resident group of geezers halfway through a game because you went to the wrong place is likely to arouse suspicion and should be avoided at all costs. Therefore, you should not only know where you're going, but you should aim to arrive at your chosen spot just before kick-off and, once there, do not move. At first, I would keep a few seats between you and the other geezers. And I would certainly advocate sitting on the end of a row if for no other reason than if they do suss you out you will be able to get away quickly. After a while, they will become familiar with you and you will be able to ease towards them until you are in their midst. If you think of David Attenborough and his documentary about living with a group of gorillas, you will get the idea. There are other ways to achieve integration more rapidly and we will come to these in the next chapter.

At some grounds, particularly in the Premier League, you will have no choice of where to sit; it will be decided for you because almost every seat will be allocated. That is the price of success. If at all possible, this is to be avoided as the people sitting around you really will have been coming for ages and will know you are a newcomer. That is unless you choose to support Arsenal, when everyone in the immediate vicinity may well be just like you.

And so, you know exactly which turnstile to use and exactly how to get to where you're going to sit. The time has come to walk through the turnstile into the magic kingdom that is about to become your home ground.

If there is a queue at your turnstile, it is always best to join it at first rather than storm to the front and draw attention to yourself outside the ground. You will be able to do this when there are a few of you and you are well known. When you get to the front, pull out the money and hand it to the man hiding in the darkened hole behind the wire-mesh screen. You will not be able to see his face and you should not try, either. The men who work turnstiles are renowned for being hideously ugly individuals who rarely venture out during daylight hours and the last thing you need is nightmares. It is also vital to remember that you must never complain about the cost of entry to the ground. Screaming out 'HOW MUCH?!' may well be the obvious thing to do, especially if you watch Chelsea, but, again, to do so would highlight your lack of match-day experience.

It is never a good idea to pass over the correct change either. Turnstile operators always throw notes on to a big pile of cash inside their darkened hole and every so often there is always the chance that you can argue that you gave him a twenty instead of a ten pound note. However, do not try this until you become a seasoned veteran, as once you start this deception you have to keep it going until someone intervenes. If you can pull it off, though, it is a good way to make some beer money. Never, ever try to use a credit card at a turnstile. For some reason, these are unacceptable to football clubs on match days and any attempt to use one will immediately mark you out as a novice.

At some games, you will not be able to pay cash on the gate; you will need to have bought a ticket. These games are called all-ticket affairs and tickets must be purchased in advance from the club. It is always worth a call during the week to see which games are all-ticket and then you will be able to experience the joy of taking time off work to travel to the club during the week to get yours. This is especially rewarding if you live miles from the club you support and have to use public transport because you have no car of your own. The only benefit here is that you can use a credit card to purchase your ticket, but the club will almost certainly load on a hefty handling charge. After all, you're only putting your hard-earned money into their pockets, so why should they incur any financial loss themselves?

If you have a ticket, as opposed to cash, the procedure at the turnstiles is simply to walk up to the gate and hand your ticket through the mesh. The operator will then tear off a portion of the ticket and violently throw the remaining part at you in the hope that it will end up on the floor. As you need this portion to show to the stewards if they get stroppy, you should be ready for this and must try to catch it, as scrabbling around amongst the various dog-ends and old chip wrappers is not only unsightly, it is hardly dignified. If a game is all-ticket, you should not try the 'I gave you a twenty' routine, as this will merely get you ejected.

During your wait to gain entry to the ground, you may well notice that some supporters will have purchased things called season tickets. These are well worth considering if you intend to make the match-day experience a regular feature of your life. They are basically books of tickets for every home game, purchased in advance at the beginning of the season. The bonus here is that you do not have to worry about obtaining tickets should your chosen club start doing well and/or make it to a cup final. The other bonus is that if you ever get your allegiance questioned, you can flash your season ticket at your inquisitor, which is almost as good a show of loyalty as your enamel badge. The downside to season-ticket ownership is that you need to take out a second mortgage at some clubs to gain one. The procedure with a season ticket at the turnstile is similar to that of the tickets. However, with a season ticket you will need to tear out the appropriate voucher for that particular match and hand it over to the man behind the mesh. Although you are supposed to, never hand over your book. Not only are turnstile operators notoriously ugly, they are hardly the most dexterous people either and it is not unknown for them to tear out a number of vouchers, meaning that you miss the next few home games. Not only that, but there is something very effeminate about carrying a little book of tickets to a game and, as a geezer, anything of this nature is to be avoided.

Once your payment or ticket has been accepted, the turnstile operator will give you a kind of grunt as recognition that you may enter the ground. Do not try and understand this grunt and never, ever ask him to repeat it. He may well become violent if you attempt to make any kind of contact with him. Having been grunted at, simply push forward and the turnstile will rotate, taking you with it. You're in.

Having negotiated the turnstile and survived the scrutiny of the operator you will now come face to face with a number of obstacles. The first of these is a member of a particular group who, although becoming rarer, still makes an appearance every so often, and he is called 'the pervert'. He – it's always a he – will invite you to lift your hands above your head so that he can run his hands over your body. He is actually supposed to be searching you for any kind of weapon, but as these searches are totally ineffective and the perverts always seem to be smiling, I have been suspicious of their motives for a number of years now. However, if someone invites you to be felt up, I mean searched, you have no choice but to comply or the Old Bill will take over and almost certainly throw you out.

After the pervert will inevitably come the programme seller, whom we have already discussed and whom you should avoid, and then someone who repeatedly shouts out 'Golden Goals, get your Golden Goals'. What he or she is actually doing is selling lottery tickets which, like all things inside grounds, are designed to extract money from you. The object of the exercise is to guess the time of the first goal, but you cannot actually guess yourself because the ticket will allocate a time to you. As this time could be anything from zero to 90 minutes and is broken down into periods of one second, the chances of actually winning are remote, and so it is far better to avoid these people and hang on to your money. At some clubs they also run a thing called a 'Lucky Number' which, like the Golden Goals, is also a kind of scam designed to relieve you of your money. Again, these people should be given a wide berth or, if you can manage it, a look of disgust. After all, they're working for the commercial machine you should learn to despise.

Having fought your way past these people, you are now free to make your way to the toilets. The way to find them is simple. Merely follow your nose or, if you have a cold, watch where every single male goes as soon as he is inside the ground. That's the toilets. This should always be your first stop, as not only have you just left the pub, but no one gets up to go to the lavatory during the game. Like at the theatre, it just isn't done. A word here about toilets at football. Firstly, never call them lavatories, the little boys' room or, for that matter, toilets. They are universally known as bogs. At half-time, you either go to the bog or you go for a slash. Nothing else. Now, if you think about it, most football grounds hold well over 15,000 people, the vast majority of whom will be male. Therefore it follows that most of them will need to go to the toilet at some time or another and, as I have just mentioned, chances are that time will be half-time. This means that the toilets will be full and you will have to queue. Do not complain about this; merely do what everyone else does and accept it. If someone talks to you, respond accordingly, but you should only ever talk about football and, more specifically, the football you have just seen (i.e. the first half). As you arrive at the front of the queue, you should get to the urinal and do your business as quickly as possible. Everyone waiting behind you will be jigging around and will be very impatient, and if the teams are back out on the pitch they will give up waiting and will do whatever they have to do where they are standing. This is not a good thing.

As you are doing your business, you will note that the walls in front of you are covered with all sorts of horrible-looking things which defy description and these should certainly not be touched under any circumstances. In fact, best not even to think about what they are or where they came from. It is also worth noting that the cubicles in football grounds should never, ever be used for the purpose for which they were designed. After all, do you really think that people would queue for the urinals when there was an empty cubicle at hand? Furthermore, very few cubicles at grounds these days actually have seats on them. They usually have bits of wood or plastic bolted to the sides of the bowl. This means that if you are forced to use them you are perched on the sides, and as a good portion of the crowd will have dampened the sides of the pan by the time you get in there, not to mention the floor, it takes very little imagination to work out that the normal rules of hygiene do not apply here. Of course, if someone else has been in there and has, for want of a better phrase, dumped their lunch before you, then the smell will be horrific, it will not have been flushed because the toilets never work and there will be no toilet paper. There is never any toilet paper in the cubicles at football grounds. No, it is better to avoid cubicles altogether. Finally, you should never wash your hands. The chances are that if you do, you will simply be adding more germs on to your skin rather than removing those already there. The best thing is not to touch anything other than yourself.

Having been to the toilet, the next stop is for refreshments, and at most grounds these facilities can be found under the stands and, somewhat ironically, right next to the toilets. We have already discussed the catering outside grounds but things are very different inside. It is far more expensive. You should never make the very simple mistake of thinking that the catering inside grounds is meant to be either tasty or nutritious; it is not. It is simply there to warm you up and, of course, to relieve you of yet more money. If you must eat, I would always recommend sweets, crisps or, if you need something warm, pies. Primarily because all of these things will come in their wrappers and therefore will be untouched by the spotty youths working behind the counter. However, here is another little tip. The cabinets used to warm the pies inside most grounds are minuscule and usually hold, at most, about 30 pies. Once these pies have been sold, which does not take long bearing in mind the average section at most grounds holds about 6,000 people, the staff will quickly replace them with cold pies. Now, as these cabinets take on average about 24 hours to heat a single pie, it does not take a genius to work out that by half-time the only pies available will be stone cold. Therefore, if you must eat, do it before the game and, as with outside, never, ever eat the hot dogs or the burgers.

Strangely, some of the hot drinks available at football grounds are usually good value. There is no real reason for this, at least not one that I can fathom, but, to be honest, the hot chocolate at most grounds is excellent. The exception when it comes to hot drinks is the tea. Never, ever drink tea at a football ground as it is invariably either powdered or, if you have the misfortune to be at a non-league ground, stewed. Indeed, if you see anyone at a football match spitting out a drink in disgust, I would almost guarantee it is tea.

If you take sugar in your drinks – always a good idea, as it disguises the aftertaste left by the water – you should not make the mistake of asking the spotty youth behind the counter for it. He, or she, will merely look at you with an expression of total bewilderment. Please note, at football grounds sugar is always in the same place. Once you have your drink, move to the end of the counter where you will find a box of sachets, most of which will be empty. Simply grab a handful and the law of averages dictates that you should get at least one with something inside. At the same time, you should also grab a thing called a stirrer. These are strips of plastic designed to stir your drink with and you will only ever find them at football grounds. They will be in the same box as the sugar and will always be at the bottom.

Strangely, as most hot drinks at football are scalding hot, they immediately melt or curl into a ball as soon as they come into contact with any kind of heat and so, with this in mind, I would always recommend you carry a pen or pencil with you. Whilst we are on the subject of hot drinks, I would always avoid any kind of soup or anything that is called either Bovril or Oxo. These are merely different types of coffee that taste of meat.

Cold drinks are another matter entirely. Cans are rarely on sale inside grounds as people have been known to throw them at players or opposing fans (perish the thought), but most clubs sell little bottles of coloured water imaginatively referred to as either cola, lemonade or cherryade. These, like most things to do with football, are viciously overpriced and, as they are kept in a cupboard next to the salmonella plate, I mean hot-dog griddle, will always be warm. To add insult to injury, the spotty oiks behind the counter will remove the lids before they give them to you and then throw them away. This, again, is in case you want to throw them at anyone. Quite why anyone would even consider throwing anything so expensive obviously escapes me, but there you are.

Finally, when talking about catering and football, the obvious question is 'Why can't I buy beer inside the ground?'. After all, seeing as the vast majority of supporters are men and most of them will have already been to a pub, surely it would make sense? Of course it would, but although it does happen at the odd ground, it will never happen at all of them. There are a number of reasons for this, but only two are really worth discussing here and they are both the fault of the police. Firstly, the availability of alcôhol would inevitably lead to supporters enjoying themselves and this would never do. Secondly, as most clubs charge 40 pence for a 24 pence Kit-Kat, can you imagine the mark-up they would put on a pint of even the cheapest lager? Even the police realise that it would be criminal and have clearly warned the clubs that it is unacceptable.

Having purchased your refreshments, you should place them into your pockets rather than carry them. The reason for this is that nothing is guaranteed to raise more mirth amongst other supporters than the sight of someone dropping their hugely expensive pie. You cannot afford to have this happen to you as you aspire to be a geezer, not a dickhead. Furthermore, if you have a hot drink, you should tip enough away to ensure that, should you trip, you will not spill any on yourself or, more importantly, another geezer. Having done all this, the time has come to make your way to your seat.

For a true geezer, one of the great experiences of match day is his first sight of the pitch. This will be heightened by the fact that by the time he gets there (i.e. late) the teams will already be on the pitch warming up and it will all be starting to happen. This is a moment to be savoured. However, for you as a novice geezer, entering the stands is fraught with danger, as it is so important. You simply have to get this part of the performance right, and this is how you should do it.

As you walk up the steps into the sunshine, the green expanse of the pitch will spread out before you and the first sounds of crowd noise will hit. This is what it's all about and you should never go directly to your seat but should always stop and take a good long look around. There are three reasons for this. The first is that you need to familiarise yourself with your surroundings to ensure that you know exactly where you are. Secondly, you need to let everyone else know that you are there because, as a geezer, you're showing out, and, finally, you should always savour this moment. The first sight of the pitch is one of the highlights of the day, and although you will have many things on your mind, you should always enjoy this moment and be seen to do so. While you are standing at the top of the steps, you should also take a long, hard look at the visitors' enclosure. All geezers do this; it is to gauge the strength of the opposition and also to spot how many geezers they have with them. After staring at them for a few seconds, you should always give a shake of your head as acknowledgement that their showing is pathetic. You should do this even if the visiting end is rammed full of geezers who are screaming for the blood of the home fans (as they will be if you are playing West Ham or Sunderland).

After a brief pause, walk down to the front of the stand using a cocky, Liam Gallagher-type walk (easily adopted by sticking out your pelvis and pulling back your shoulders). At the bottom of the steps, stop and turn around to face the crowd. If you have the nerve, you could wave to an imaginary friend (you never know, one day someone may even wave back) or even say hello to a few people (well, not hello, more 'all right?'). As everyone who goes to football likes to be recognised, they will always reply and may even ask you something about the forthcoming game. As all of your actions are designed to let anyone watching you know that you have been there before, actually talking to someone is a very good way to show that you are a long-term fan. Therefore conversations are to be encouraged. However, they should be kept very short as you may be talking to an anorak or even an old git, which would damage your status immediately. Never talk to women inside grounds. They should not even be there.

One thing you should not do at this point is to acknowledge the players. This should only be done once you have extreme confidence in your own performance and should, in most cases, be derogatory. For example, if an opposing player looks at you, you should immediately give him the 'V' sign and a sneer of hatred (we will discuss both players and these actions in the next chapter). This is not designed to upset him, but simply to endear you to the other geezers. You should not, at this point, insult your own players. The reason for this is that most geezers have their favourites amongst the team and to insult one of them could well undo all of the good work already carried out. It is far better to bide your time and work out who the home geezers admire and who they dislike before hurling any insults of your own. Furthermore, should a ball come near you as you are standing at the bottom of the stands, you should never, ever touch it. There is always the chance that you will do something stupid and it is simply not worth the risk at this point.

Having paused, waved and possibly spoken to someone or abused a visiting player, walk back up the steps using your Liam Gallagher-type walk and take your seat. If you've timed it right, the players are about to go off the pitch. Do not be alarmed by this; you have not missed anything. It is simply that they have been warming up and are about to go off and get their playing kit on. Once they have done this, they will reappear. The game is only minutes away.

Chapter Nine

The Game

An empty football ground is a sad place. It is merely a hollow shell devoid of any kind of life or passion. On match days, however, everything changes. The football ground explodes into life and, unless you're a Spurs or L*t*n fan (but that's your own fault), is truly a joy to be in. Football fans give it that life and you, having negotiated the turnstiles, toilets and food, are now a part of that. Never forget that geezers are, above all else, football fans.

Having arrived at your seat just in time to watch the teams walk off the field after their warm-up, you should now take a few seconds to familiarise yourself with your surroundings. You will already know that the main crop of geezers are just feet away from where you're sitting and you will also know where the opposing fans are. There are, however, a few other things you need to note. The first of these is that cameras are watching your every move. No, not those of BSkyB or the BBC, but of the Old Bill. Inside a ground, closed circuit television (CCTV) will monitor your every move, which is the main reason why you should behave yourself. These cameras will be located in the roof of the stands, and although you need to know where they are, you should not stare into them nor pull faces if they are looking at you. This is not because you will upset anyone, but because people sitting near you will think you a twat. There will, of course, be other cameras inside the ground and these really are from BSkyB or the BBC. They will be concerned solely with watching the game, not you. You should also make a note of where these are so that when your team is on you may well be able to see yourself on the television. Do not, under any circumstances, wave at these cameras. Hurling abuse or making obscene gestures is fine, but being seen waving and grinning on *Match of the Day* is not the stuff geezers are made of. As you look around, you should also look out for the location of the loudspeakers used to make announcements. This is because before they arrived at your ground they were almost certainly used at an Iron Maiden concert and no one has ever known how to turn the sound down. If you value your hearing at all, never sit directly in front of them.

Finally, you need to make a mental note of where the stewards and policemen are standing so that you can avoid any problems later on or, if things go wrong, you can ask them to get you out of there fairly rapidly. We have already talked about the role of the stewards and the police outside grounds, but inside they are a different proposition altogether, and so before we carry on we should take another brief look at them.

Unlike outside grounds, where they are merely an irritation, inside grounds stewards turn into a major pain in the arse. This is because they actually do have a degree of power and they certainly do like to use it if they can. There are a number of ways this can be achieved. For example, if a game is all-ticket, they will often come into the crowd and ask to see your ticket stub on the pretext that you are sitting in the wrong seat. In fact they have little or no interest in your seat number but are merely trying to irritate you. Similarly, stewards are often placed at strategic points around the pitch, their supposed role being to stop fans getting on to the field of play and arguing with a player or official who may have done something contrary to the game plan employed by your team. However, rather than watch the crowd, they tend to watch the game – which not only renders them totally ineffective but also means that they are standing directly in front of someone. Do not be deceived by the blank expressions on their faces; this is another tactic designed to irritate supporters and it always works.

But the main function of stewards inside a ground, and the one for which they are universally loathed, is to act as a grass. What this means is that if a steward spots someone doing something he thinks they should not be doing (i.e. enjoying themselves) or if he merely takes exception to the face of a certain individual, he will report them to the police. This is called 'grassing them up'. Once this happens, the following sequence of events will occur: within seconds, no matter what the nature of the incident, hordes of policemen will descend on the area. Rather than ascertain the facts before acting, they will simply barge their way through the crowd, upsetting all and sundry, until they arrive in the approximate vicinity of the offending individual. Once there, having upset everyone within 50 feet, they will reach out and grab the nearest person under five foot three and proceed to drag him out of the area. This will, in turn, infuriate every other supporter in the ground and tempers will rise. Then, as the innocent party (or, on very rare occasions, guilty party) is dragged out kicking and screaming, abuse will rain down on both policemen and stewards, ensuring that the local papers will be full of letters from angry fans throughout the coming week. Throwing people out seems to be the only role policemen have inside grounds.

Now, if you ever have the misfortune to be thrown out of a ground, do not despair. It can, in fact, be a good thing. If it does happen, you must make sure that you do everything you can to maximise its value to you as a geezer. The way to do this is to ensure that everyone sees that it is you getting dragged out by being as vocal and abusive as possible. You can also thrash about a bit if you like. This will earn you instant fame amongst your peers and you will immediately be known as 'the bloke who got thrown out against . . .'. This instant fame can be taken to even greater heights if you are dragged out across the front of the visitors' enclosure. If this happens, you should thrash about a bit more and hurl abuse at them as you are escorted out. They will hurl abuse back and all the geezers from your side will see this and think you are a hero. It never fails. If you can achieve this during an actual game, especially when the television cameras are on, all the better. There is always the chance that your actions will be seen on television and you may even get the opportunity to hurl abuse at a player.

Getting thrown out of a ground is as good as a rite of passage for geezers. They have all experienced it at some time or another and everyone remembers the first time. Do not worry about obtaining a criminal record as a result of your ejection. Most policemen will merely throw you out and close the door behind you as they do not want to miss the game. However, if you are unlucky enough to be dragged out by an officer of the law who takes his job seriously, then simply grovelling to his better nature invariably works.

Before we continue, there is one other thing you should think about: mobile phones. You would never dream of walking into the Albert Hall with your phone turned on, and the same thing applies at a football ground. In fact, you shouldn't even have it with you. As you are a geezer, everyone should know where you are on a match day and the last thing in the world they should even think about doing is disturbing you. If you must maintain a link with the outside world then carry a pager, but keep it hidden and make sure that anyone likely to call you knows that you will not be ringing them back. Inevitably, given their explosion amongst the general public, you will see a number of people talking into mobiles during games, especially at half-time. If they are sads, then what else can you expect, but if they are clearly geezers then they are hooligans. You should not approach nor talk to these people. We will talk about them later.

Okay. The next 90 minutes are what it's all about and so as you sit there, waiting for the teams to come out on to the pitch, you will become aware of an aura of anticipation. This is caused by all of the anoraks, old gits, sads and scum straining at the leash to catch the first glimpse of their team. Geezers do not do this. Geezers remain aloof, talking amongst themselves or, if they are really smooth, reading the paper or a borrowed programme. The first time a geezer takes any obvious notice of his surroundings is when the two teams leave the tunnel and walk out on to the pitch. At this point, the anoraks will stand and throw huge amounts of waste paper in the air (most of which will be yellow and torn from old copies of the Yellow Pages) or throw toilet rolls at the goalkeepers. The noise level will also increase markedly and then, and only then, will the geezers put away their papers, stand up and clap their boys out on to the pitch. From then on, as a geezer, you will remain standing until half-time.

With the teams on the pitch, it is only natural that you will begin to feel excited. This is not a bad thing. Football is, after all, exciting and let's face it, you are there because you enjoy it. However, this joy is not because you are at football, it is because you are in the presence of your team. And it is *your* team. You are, or aspire to be, a part of the culture that is your club. That means, as I have already said, that the soul of the club is a part of you, or, to look at it another way, you are a part of it. As a geezer, your attitude towards players should reflect this. To you, they are merely representing your club. Although they may be wearing the shirt, they are not a part of it as you are. After all, they could be sold tomorrow, or badly injured, and so they would merely be replaced with someone else. But you, well, you are there for ever. Well, at least from now on. Fair enough, if players run their hearts out, they are deemed worthy of all the adulation you can give them, but if they give anything less than 110 per cent then they have let you down and that is unforgivable. Anoraks worship players; geezers merely tolerate them – but only while they wear your shirt.

As the game progresses, you should begin to notice the singing, the chanting and the language. These are some of the great attractions of football, but for you, the wannabe geezer, they are fraught with danger. There is nothing more embarrassing than adding on that extra 'Come on you 'Orns' just as everyone else has finished.

It is true to say that football songs come in many forms; some are supportive, some are abusive and some are downright disgusting but they all have one thing in common: they are all initially impossible to decipher. You must exercise extreme caution here. The key is to listen and, if you can, to lip-read. Never join in if you don't know the words and, above all, never, ever ask what those words are. It will mean certain death. However, as most football songs are based around pop tunes, the actual melody should not be too difficult to pin down, and from then on it's just a matter of filling in the words. Indeed, until you know the basics, you can always mime or even grunt along until the lyrics become clearer. In fact, some football fans only ever grunt. Some clubs have songs that have been adopted as signature tunes and if you are at some such club these songs should be learnt as quickly as possible. It will not be too difficult to discover which tunes these are, as they will be sung over and over again. For example, at Liverpool it's 'You'll Never Walk Alone' and at West Ham it's 'I'm Forever Blowing Bubbles'. You should note, however, that 'We're shit, and we know we are' is not the anthem of the L★t★n T★wn fans. Even if it is true. To help you out, I have written the lyrics of a number of tunes at the back of the book, but you should remember that not all of these will be sung at your own club. Again, be wary and you will be fine.

On a similar vein, the chanting at football should be given a great deal of attention if for no other reason than it is invariably funny. References to sexual practices are the norm and these should be positively encouraged. Telling a player that his girlfriend enjoys anal sex with animals or that his mum performed oral sex on you only last night may not, on the face of it, hold much humour, but inside a stadium on match day they are highly amusing phrases. Until you have been accepted into the fold, however, I would not recommend that you shout anything out on your own. Your sense of humour may be totally different from everyone else's and you have to avoid drawing attention to yourself initially. Obviously, some of the chanting you will hear at football will be directed at the officials, but I have never agreed with this and would urge you not to do it. Not only is it pointless (I have yet to see a referee have a go at the crowd as a result of such abuse) but it is also counter-productive. By this I simply mean that if you were a linesman and the home crowd had been giving you 89 minutes of stick for being bald, fat or a combination of both, would you throw up your flag to give the visiting striker offside if there were any doubt at all? I rest my case.

Whilst singing and chanting are one thing, the vocabulary used at football is something else entirely. Truth to tell, it has little to do with the actual game as it is invariably abusive, but this is one of the reasons why you are there and hurling abuse is expected of you. It will quickly become apparent that most of the abuse you hear coming from the other geezers will be directed at the visiting supporters, or scum. That is, after all, one of the reasons why they have been allowed into your ground. There is an art to hurling abuse at other fans and it takes a great deal of time to master, but the majority of the content will be historical, geographical or stereotypical. For example: every club south of L*t*n are cockneys, all supporters from the north-east are Geordies and all scousers live in slums and eat rats. People from Manchester are all thieving bastards or drug dealers, all northerners are unemployed, have stupid haircuts and ridiculous moustaches, whilst all southern males are mouthy and every woman from London is a slag.

If you feel the need to abuse players (and who doesn't?) then like every other aspect of geezerdom it should be treated with extreme caution if you are to avoid drawing attention to yourself. As a basic rule of thumb, visiting players should never be called by their actual names but should always be referred to as either wanker, cunt or, if they have long hair, gypo. Furthermore, if they are Welsh they are druids, if they are Irish they are thick (and referred to as Mick) or if they are Scottish they are both ugly and tight-fisted. No footballer has a father. As regards the players of your own side, they should always be called by their full surname. Never use their nickname or their Christian name, as this is what anoraks do. For example, whilst an anorak would shout, 'Come on, Gazza, pull your socks up,' a geezer would scream, 'Gascoigne! You cunt! Get your lazy arse in gear, for fuck's sake!' You should also avoid any reference to the actual mechanics of the game, as this may well show up your total lack of footballing knowledge. Therefore, such phrases as 'Why isn't Batty playing slightly deeper today?' will rarely pass your lips, whilst 'Oi! Batty, you're a fucking idiot!' (or some such variation) almost certainly will. You should never, however, hurl any kind of racist abuse at players or, for that matter, opposing supporters. Not only is it not very nice, it is also illegal and is highly likely to earn you a very well-deserved slap. Not only from anyone within hitting distance who is black but also from the other geezers who are invariably above such things.

There are a number of subjects which provide ammunition for the abuse of players and these should be explored before the game to ensure that you are well armed. One such area is their playing history. For example, if a certain player was transferred from your club at any time during his career, he is a reject. If he left because he refused to sign a new contract, he is a greedy bastard, and if he ever played for your local rivals, he is referred to as scum and should be booed every time he touches the ball. An opposing player should also be abused if he did anything to upset the home fans during a previous game. If this happens, you should not join in with it as you were not there so you do not know what it's all about, and you should certainly never ask. Players will also earn the wrath of the opposing supporters if they have ever appeared in the tabloids for anything other than football at any time in their lives. I will not point out some of the more obvious examples here, but think of pop singers, drink, wives, illegal substances, driving and prisons and you will get some idea. If, however, one of your players appears in the daily papers, such things merely make him more interesting.

Finally, opposition players should be abused if they have the temerity to make gestures to the crowd. One of the ironies of football fandom is that you, as a fan, can spend 90 minutes abusing an individual but if they make a single demonstration of hostility or even good humour in the direction of anyone in the entire crowd, the geezers in particular will be incensed. If this happens, it is your duty to vent your outrage at this player as he has overstepped the mark. Indeed, some would even argue that complaints should be made to the police, but that is best left to the anoraks who, if the gesture was abusive, will almost certainly be reduced to tears.

You should also note that players of opposing sides never do anything that is any good. If a rival player exhibits skill that draws gasps of admiration from the anoraks, you will invariably hear a geezer remark that he is merely a lucky cunt and that they do that every Sunday morning when they play for their pub side. This is called bravado or, to use a better term, bullshit. You will hear lots of this during every single game you will ever attend. The bottom line here is that no opposing player should ever be given praise for a single thing he does on the pitch in front of you. It matters not if it's a penalty save or a 30-yard volley into the top of the net, whatever he does is detrimental to your own team and therefore is to be criticised. The same approach should also be taken in the unlikely event of your own team exhibiting any kind of skill. That is, after all, why they are out there and why they get paid so much money. There are always exceptions to this, of course. For example, if your goalkeeper scores directly from a goal kick he should be applauded. However, generally speaking, if your midfield general hits a 35-yard screamer through a crowd of players and into the net, the phrase 'About fucking time the idle cunt did something!' will almost certainly ring out from amongst the geezers once the celebrations have died down.

If a goal is scored, your response will obviously depend on who scored it and at what stage in the game it came. However, as a rule of thumb, if your own team scores, at all, then the response is, quite simply, to go mad. After all, football is all about scoring goals and if your lads do it, it should be celebrated. Jumping up and down, waving your arms about, screaming and even running around like some demented banshee are all legitimate celebrations and you will not be ridiculed if you do any of these (primarily because everyone else will be doing something similar). After about 30 seconds of this, the mood changes to one of aggressive relief. By this I mean that you should calm down a bit and, with clenched fists, merely repeat the word 'yes' over and over again through clenched teeth. After about ten seconds of this you should indulge in a bit of back-slapping with your mates before turning your attention to the opposition supporters and a bit of abuse hurling. It is, however, important to note that whilst you are indeed celebrating a goal, you are not simply pouring adulation on the scorer. The fact that someone has actually done his job and put the ball in the net, no matter how it was done, is not the only cause for celebration here. Far more important is the fact that this goal will have pissed off the other side and their fans. The two things that are, with the exception of being with other geezers and having a laugh, the true reasons for going to football.

Whilst this is the standard routine for all geezers when their team scores, there are exceptions. But only two. Firstly, if a goal is scored in a game that is of extraordinary importance, such as a local derby or a cup-tie, then the level of celebration should be increased just a tad. Secondly, if your team are getting hammered and the goal is simply a fluke, then polite applause is all that is necessary, although this should be accompanied by the hurling of abuse at the scorer who should have been putting in more of an effort. For you, as a wannabe geezer, goals are a godsend. The moment that ball hits the net, all the other geezers will explode in a frenzy of relief and/or jubilation. This will enable you to show that you are as much a supporter as they are by going equally mental and dispelling at a stroke any doubts they may have about your allegiance.

Sadly, it is inevitable that sooner or later someone will score against your team. For some, this will come more frequently than for others (see Manchester City). When this happens, be it to equalise or to give them the lead, the normal response is to stand up, turn around to face the back of the stand, look to either the heavens or the floor and then swear. A lot. You should then pour scorn on your entire team and then the manager, who should have made sure this did not happen. That is, after all, his job. If the goal has come about as a result of poor refereeing or a dubious decision by a linesman, then abuse should rain down on the officials. Once this has been done, the geezers will turn their attentions to the opposing fans and for the next five minutes will hurl abuse at them if for no other reason than it will make them feel better. The opposing fans will, of course, be much too happy to notice this. If the opposing team score to close the gap on your own boys (i.e. to make it 2–1 or 3–2) then the same action should be taken but to a lesser degree, whilst if their goal is purely token (i.e. to make it 4–1, 5–1, etc.) then you should merely shake your head. If the goal is a last-minute or injury-time winner, especially in a match against your local rivals, then the actions are simple: merely think about the worst thing that has ever happened to you, magnify it by ten and react accordingly. If you can cry to order, this is the time to do it.

In between the goals or, in the case of Tottenham and Shit Town, instead of the goals, there will be long periods where the only thing to occupy you is the game, the singing or the abusing. This is all well and good, but on a cold day something is needed to help people to keep warm. This is especially important now that the terraces are consigned to history at most grounds and you have to sit down. Therefore, to ensure that the blood is kept flowing in order to aid the avoidance of hypothermia, the crowd, and in particular the geezers, either clap their hands to accompany the songs or use a series of movements or gestures. These have evolved not only to complement the verbal abuse but also as a form of ridicule in their own right. However, although these gestures take many forms, they have, unlike the vocal forms of communication, become fairly standardised. This is because both sets of fans need to know what the other is saying to them. Almost all of the gestures you will see inside and outside grounds are described at the back of this book.

Strangely, given the amount of singing and movement inside stadia, dancing has never really caught on at football. There is no real reason for this. Although it is beginning to change now that most grounds play music after every goal, it is still a rarity. The one major exception is at West Bromwich Albion, where the supporters, and in particular the geezers, have adopted an odd frolic called 'boinging'. This is achieved by simply bouncing up and down whilst chanting 'boing, boing Baggies' over and over again. I have to say it is quite humorous, but it should not be attempted at your own club as you will almost certainly attract heaps of abuse and ridicule because you will be doing it on your own.

After about 45 minutes, the referee will blow the whistle for half-time and the players will troop off the pitch to either rapturous applause or heaps of abuse, depending on how they have done in the first half. During this interval, known universally simply as half-time, the crowd will break into quiet conversation. All singing, chanting and abusing will cease, as it is not only the players who need a rest. At this point, you can, if you wish, sit down. However, having been in the pub before the game and having possibly also drunk at least one hot drink as you made your way to your seat, you may well need to go to the toilet. If you need to do this, fine, but remember all the information I provided earlier. Alternatively, you may fancy something to eat or drink, and, again, this is fine. However, given the fact that everyone and his dog will have the same idea, you should not plan on doing both, as you only have a few minutes.

Other things may also take place during this break, as clubs seem to believe that supporters need entertaining during half-time. This 'entertainment' could be anything from cheerleaders (which sounds attractive but the girls are usually under 11 and are invariably ugly and/or fat) or penalty shoot-outs between local schools (and just why should they be on the pitch and not you?) to some local celebrity lording it up and talking bollocks. As a geezer, all half-time entertainment is to be ignored and/or ridiculed. The one and only thing of any importance that takes place between the two periods of play is the reading out of the other half-time scores. As these are read out, the geezers will cheer or boo depending on the relevant score. This is done merely to show who they like and who they do not. You should not join in here until you know which clubs are in favour amongst the other geezers, as you may well make a major mistake.

You must be back at your seat by the time the teams come out on to the pitch for the second half as it is your duty to clap your lads out and begin the hurling of abuse at the opposition. As soon as the game starts, the cycle of singing and abusing should simply be repeated, as per the first period. However, as time passes, you will notice that things will become a little more heated, especially if your lads are not winning or are hanging on for dear life.

With about ten minutes of the game remaining, you will almost certainly start to notice a number of people leaving the game early. Quite why these people do this is one of football's great mysteries. Even those who do it cannot explain why, although it is generally believed that they are infected with some kind of mental disease. Never, ever do this. Even if your team are getting the thrashing of all time. The reason for this is that not only is there the chance you may miss something exciting, but also that as a geezer, once the whistle has blown to end the game, it is your duty either to clap your lads off the pitch or to hurl even more abuse at them for letting you down.

Once the final whistle is blown to end the game, the geezers will begin to talk about the match. Almost certainly for the first time. However, rather than any form of conversation, this discussion will in fact be a series of short sentences which are more announcements than statements, for example 'Lee is fucking useless', 'Bazeley was the dog's bollocks today' or 'They were the worst team we've had here all year'. Do not try to make in-depth observations about offside traps or diamond formations, as everyone will look at you as if you are a twat. As they do this, the geezers will make their way out of the ground and you should go with them. However, rather than walk along the gangways, any geezer worth his salt (and that's all of them) will walk directly over the seats to take the most direct way out of the ground. This is designed not only to get out, and therefore into the pub, more rapidly, but also to irritate everyone else stupid enough to queue. Again, this is fraught with danger for those not used to doing it because walking over seats is not only undignified, it can also be highly dangerous. After all, falling arse-over-tit in front of hordes of other geezers and anoraks will not do your credibility any good, will it? It is, therefore, best to practise this at home if you can. Simply line up every chair you have in the house and walk backwards and forwards over them until you can do it in some degree of safety. Believe me, it will be worth it.

Once you have negotiated the seats, make your way to the exit and then out into the street. At this point you may well come into close contact with some of the opposing fans for the first time, but you should not talk to them under any circumstances. Not only have you been hurling abuse at each other for the last hour and a half, but if they are celebrating a victory they may well be gloating, which means they will be getting one over on you. Conversely, if you are celebrating, you will be gloating, which, although totally acceptable on the face of it, may well earn you a smack in the mouth. This is to be avoided at all costs.

Having left the ground, the next step is entirely dependent on what happened during the game. If you managed to make any kind of contact with other geezers, then after a bit of self-congratulation make your way to the pub with them and get drinking. But be wary, especially if it is your first game amongst the geezers. Remember the golden rule and never, ever ponce off others. After all, real geezers know when to put their hands in their pockets and get their round in. Furthermore, do not stay too long and do not get drunk. You never know what you will say if you are smashed, and to blow your cover after achieving so much would be tragic. And so at this stage it is simply not worth it. There will be plenty of other times.

If you failed to make any real inroads with the other geezers, then it's best to give the pub a miss. However, you should not despair. Not only have you survived your first game amongst your peers, but others will have certainly noticed your presence. Next time they may well welcome you with open arms. Believe me, if you got this far and survived without being found out, you're halfway there. Gaining acceptance is only a matter of time.

Part Three
On the Road

Chapter Ten

Travelling Away

Having survived your first home game intact, you may well decide that going to an away game is a good idea. And it is. It is no exaggeration to say that when you eventually become a 100 per cent geezer, some of the best days you will have as you support your lads will be when you travel with them to some god-forsaken ground at the other end of the country. From such trips, legends are born.

One of the reasons for this is that as you travel, you will spend more time in the company of the other geezers. Being stuck in a coach, car, van or even on a train with loads of other blokes is a great way to get to know them. Not only that but, as you travel, you will be able to act even louder, cockier and flasher than when you are at home. Confident in the knowledge that if you do upset anyone, you need not be that concerned because you will almost certainly never see them again. This, as an attraction, should not be underestimated.

However, as a novice geezer, I would urge a degree of caution before you make the decision to travel to an away fixture. It is never a good idea to travel on your own. Not only can it be very dangerous at certain clubs, it is also very sad. It is far better, not to mention safer, to go with another group of geezers. And, let's face it, as you are still learning your craft, that should be one of the ultimate goals. Therefore much will depend on what happened when you walked through those home turnstiles for the very first time. If you managed to make contact with other geezers, it is better to take your time and get to know them in the hope that they will eventually invite you to travel with them. If you failed to meet anyone at your first game, I would advise you simply to persevere with the home fixtures for now. Eventually you will get there. If you are impatient, however, and the need to travel is great, there is a way round this, but it is fraught with danger. I will discuss it later.

When you do eventually decide to travel, whoever it is with, you need to decide how to do it and that means transport. This can be obtained in any number of ways and so before we get into the nitty gritty we need to have a look at some of the various forms available.

In the golden days of geezerdom, that is, the late '70s and early '80s, most travel was achieved courtesy of British Rail. At that time, in an effort to get as many of their own fans as possible to games, most clubs hired their own trains for away trips. These were known as 'specials'. Rammed with geezers, most of whom were the worse for wear for drink, they often took on the appearance of a St Trinian's School outing and were absolutely brilliant things to be on. Inter-compartment fights were routine ways of passing the time, as was throwing empty crisp packets full of urine out of the window as you sped through a train station on your journey. Not only that, but a trainload of geezers pulling into a station was a fearsome sight to behold.

Leaving aside the hazards associated with flying faeces, there were various problems surrounding the 'specials', most of which involved hooliganism. The first was that most train stations are miles away from the local stadium and all the supporters would have to walk to the ground, which usually meant passing through the town centre. This led to all kinds of trouble for the police, usually involving fighting. Not only that, but rail stations, particularly mainline stations such as Euston and King's Cross, became battlegrounds every Saturday night as groups converged on them from all points of the compass. The other problem with the hooligans – and in the early '80s most football fans were hooligans in some form or another – was that they invariably ended up wrecking the trains. This led to British Rail getting the right hump and scrapping the 'specials', a decision that was to herald the end of an era.

Nowadays, large numbers of fans still travel by rail to away games but it has become so expensive that it is hardly viable.

Especially as it is almost impossible to jump the train without buying a ticket (bloody inspectors). However, there are a few advantages the train does have over every other form of transport, the main one being that you can move thousands of geezers at a time. Not only that, but most trains have food and drink on board. Expensive food and drink, I grant you, but at least you can get it. This means that as long as the journey is long enough, and you have the funds, you can get shit-faced, have a sleep and then sober up. All in a few hours. You can also play cards, read or even have a good old sing-song on the train if you feel like it, and you should not discount the odd opportunity to pull on the journey. But we'll talk about that later.

Personally, I do not like going to football by rail these days. As someone who remembers legendary trips on football specials, the sanitised compartments we have on trains today are not for me. No, it's far better to travel by road – and there are, of course, myriad ways to do this.

The car is, of course, the most obvious. Most of us have them and those who do not can usually gain access to them. Indeed, hiring a car is an excellent way to get to away games because not only will it be reasonably cheap, the costs being shared four ways, but if you break down or anything happens to the motor it isn't your problem.

The advantages of the car are clear. You can listen to the radio, smoke to your heart's content, eat, stop wherever you feel like it and even sleep if you want, although this is not to be recommended if you are driving. And if you can you should avoid driving on an away trip at all costs. You see, whilst the true geezer will always pay his way and stand his round without any prompting from anyone, leaving another geezer's car looking like a shit hole after a four-hour trip seems to be obligatory. I speak from bitter experience here. And not only that but, as the driver, you will not be able to drink, every other person in that car will have no problem falling asleep within seconds of setting off for home (leaving you to survive the journey alone and on Pro-plus and excessive nicotine) and if you do have the misfortune to break down it will be your fault and you will have to walk to the nearest phone.

The other downsides to travelling in a car are that you can only take a total of four or, at best, five people. At least one of them will feel sick or have the trots at some time or another and all of them will suffer from excessive wind. And someone will always sneak in some egg sandwiches and open them before anyone else realises. Much the same thing can be said of the minibus, although the problems of wind and egg-sandwich abuse are magnified fifteen-fold. Not only that but a minibus will be slower.

If you do travel by car or minibus, there are a few things you should not do. Primarily these are to avoid any problems with the locals as you get near to the ground or leave it parked up. The most obvious is to refrain from doing anything that shows which club you follow. As a geezer you know who you support and it isn't anyone else's damn business. Anoraks have scarves hanging out of windows; geezers don't. Similarly, stickers along the lines of 'Don't follow me, follow Watford' should be avoided at all costs, as should any kind of banner, as one of the locals may take exception to them with obvious consequences. You should also avoid picking up hitch-hikers. You have no idea who they are or, more importantly, who they support. They could even be an old git, and once they are in that car you're stuck with them.

If you are forced to drive, I would always recommend that you hire a van. By doing this you can isolate yourself from the other geezers, and therefore the smell, by hiring one with a bulkhead. You can also cause them a great deal of distress by not stopping when they need the toilet, driving quickly around corners and dancing on the brakes like Wayne Sleep on heat. For the passengers, vans have a number of advantages over other forms of transport, one of which is that those in the back can drink to their heart's content. However, even this delightful feature pales into insignificance when compared to their most appealing attribute of all. You see, pulling up in a van, throwing open the back doors and disgorging 15 geezers into the street sure scares the shit out of the locals.

A word of warning here about going to the toilet on your travels. If you do have to urinate, it isn't a problem as you can do it anywhere. Within the realms of decency, of course. However, if you have to lighten your load, you should always ensure that you stop at either a motorway services or a café. The reason for this is that squatting down is not only undignified, it can also be a dangerous activity. If it's dark, you do not know what is underneath you, nor who is watching. And, of course, you will need paper, and if you've forgotten it do you really think your mates will get it for you? They will be too involved with finding things to throw at you in the hope that you will soil your trousers. You should never, ever wipe your backside on anything you find by the side of the road. Many a serious injury has been caused by inadvertent contact with a stinging nettle, and if you were a bee working away inside a flower and someone shat on you, how would you feel? If the need to evacuate your stomach is desperate, it is always worth using something like a crisp packet or a sandwich bag. If you do that, you can always throw it at someone as you drive along.

I should also warn you about parking, as this is another aspect of away travel that can be especially dangerous. Always avoid multi-storey car parks. Not only are they notoriously expensive, but if the locals get the hump with you for some reason, there is no escape. Similarly, you should avoid the club car park if they have one. Parking there means that you will have to walk amongst the home fans and they may well take exception to that if your lads have just dealt out a stuffing.

Side streets are always a good bet, although it is always best to choose one near to the away end. Again, this will avoid any problems with the local geezers. Side streets, however, can hold a specific problem of their own, especially in Liverpool or Manchester: kids. If, as you park your car, minibus or van, a kid comes up to you and offers, for a small fee, to look after your vehicle while you are at the game, you should always, always accept the offer. If you do not, he will merely cause damage to it when you are out of sight. While this may not concern you if it is a hire car, if he slashes the tyres you will be in the shit and who needs that? The ideal way to deal with this is to tell him that you will pay him half now and half when you get back. That way, the chances are that he really will keep an eye on it for you. If he agrees, you should always pay up. He may well be a demon with a half-brick.

Of course, if there are enough geezers and you all travel together regularly, you can always go by coach. This is an excellent form of transport and is highly recommended. Not only can you move 50 plus geezers at a time, but most modern coaches are also extremely comfortable. They also have televisions on board. This will allow you to watch loads of footie, comedy or even porno films as you travel along. Now, as someone who does not really like porn, I have to say that on footie coaches it is a good idea. Not for any personal pleasure, you understand, but because cars following will be able to see the screen and the reaction from them can often prove to be hilarious. Many a crash has been caused by Mr and Mrs Average witnessing someone performing oral sex whilst travelling up the M1. The other advantage to coaches is, of course, that they have toilets on board. This will prevent that feeling of agony as your bladder reaches bursting point from drinking too many cans of lager before you set off. However, a word of caution. The toilets on coaches are tiny cubicles and the same rules apply as for the cubicles inside grounds. Additionally, everyone else on the coach will know that the stench infecting the entire vehicle came from you.

If you do travel by coach, you will soon note that the Old Bill will take more than a passing interest in you. This is because they will know who you are and where you are going, so they will do everything in their (considerable) power to make sure that you go directly to the ground as soon as you come within their boundaries. This will inevitably mean that they stop you in a lay-by and keep you there for hours on end. They will also make sure that you have no alcohol on board as this is illegal (tragic!) and will either confiscate it or turn you away. They may even do both. To avoid this you should ensure that if you do want to stop for a drink, you do so in a town on the way. This can only be achieved through the good nature of your coach driver, who should be offered excessive bribes to ensure that he agrees to do this.

Earlier, I briefly mentioned that there is a way to get to an away game on your own if you are really desperate. However, for anyone who aspires to be a geezer, I repeat my warning that it is very dangerous and not to be undertaken lightly. If it all goes wrong, and there is every chance that it will, any credibility you have built up amongst the other geezers will vanish at a stroke. You see, if you really must travel and there is no other way to get there – and I must grudgingly applaud you if you are that desperate – then you simply have to go on the club coach.

These are to be avoided because they are run by the club and, like all things to do with them, are designed to relieve you of money. Not only that, but they will be rammed full of anoraks, old gits and even women and kids. They will also be bedecked in banners, flags, scarves and even teddy bears dressed in the club colours. Furthermore, they will not stop *en route*, especially not for any alcoholic refreshments, the video will be broken and the driver will hate football so will refuse to listen to Radio Five.

If this very last resort is all you have, however, and you still dream of a life of geezerdom, then you simply have to avoid being seen at all costs. The way to do this is to simply get on the coach as quickly as you can and lie low until you get to the ground. You should also ensure that you do not talk to anyone. This is because, as I mentioned earlier, everyone on that bus will be beneath you as a geezer and you cannot afford to let them think you like them. After all, there is always the chance that they may spot you at another game and come up and start talking to you as if you were a long-lost friend. You cannot afford for that to happen.

If, by some miracle, the coaches decide to stop somewhere, do not get off in case you are spotted. Simply feign sleep and everyone will ignore you. Once you arrive at your destination, be the last off the coach and get as far away from the anoraks as quickly as you possibly can. At this point you need to find other geezers from your own club, and if they recognise you they will hopefully think you came by rail. If they don't, however, you could be in big trouble as they may well think you are one of the opposition. That's just one of the risks, I'm afraid.

If you make it into the ground unscathed, you may well be able to blag yourself a lift home, which is an excellent way to get in with the other geezers. If this happens, though, make sure that you concoct a reasonably believable story to explain how you arrived at the ground in the first place. You should also ensure that you recognise the person who is offering you the lift home. After all, being taken home to Birmingham is no joke if you live in Northampton. If you receive no offer of a lift, you will need to get back to the club coaches. This may prove more difficult than when you arrived because, as a result of police influence, all the geezers' coaches will be parked with the club ones. The best thing to do here is to walk up to where the coaches are parked and simply wander around for a while before diving on to your coach and hiding until you pull away. As I said, it's a dangerous ploy. When you arrive home, simply get off the coach and get away as quickly as you can. You just have to hope that no one spotted you.

There are, of course, a number of other ways to get to away games but in the main these are not really worth considering, although in the interests of fairness we should take a brief look at them. After all, if you're stuck, a true geezer will get to a game no matter what.

As a biker of sorts, the idea of riding to an away game does appeal to me a great deal. Indeed, most bikers need little by way of an excuse to travel anywhere on their machines and football is as good a reason as any. However, on the downside, not only is it highly likely to rain, especially if you go up north, but you also have to carry all that clothing around with you all day – and crash helmets are hardly the most stylish of accessories, are they? You will also be on your own because no true biking bloke carries passengers.

Aircraft should be avoided if you are staying in this country. After all, travel is one of the great features of geezerdom and a four-hour coach trip holds a good deal more attraction than a visit to two airports and a wait at a taxi rank. Much the same thing can be said of helicopters, although, it has to be said, they are flash and in any other circumstances are a great way to get about. The other method of transport which should be avoided at all costs is thumbing or hitch-hiking. This is a non-starter for any number of reasons, the main one being that over the years there have been numerous instances of football fans being hijacked by rival fans and taken to games with other clubs. And who wants that? There is also the chance that you will be beaten up and robbed, which is hardly a good thing either.

Finally, a quick word about the London Underground. This most necessary of evils is unavoidable if you want to travel to a game in the capital and do not want to do it by road. Make no mistake, the tube can be a dangerous place to be. Not only do you have to run the gauntlet of various beggars, buskers and lunatics, but the tube map has been specially designed over the years to ensure that people from outside the capital have as much difficulty finding their way around as possible. Indeed, as we speak, there are probably thousands of Japanese tourists circulating on the Circle Line, desperate to get off. Saturdays are even worse. Football fans from all over the country head for the West End as if it were some kind of Mecca and then, after consuming huge amounts of very expensive alcohol, they head for their respective venues. Or at least try to.

If they do actually manage to navigate the system and make it to their game, they then head back into the centre afterwards for more alcohol. Although there is nothing wrong with that, the fly in the ointment is the fact that those firms who follow the London clubs actually do know their way around the tube network and they certainly use it to their advantage. Every time you pull into a station, you do not know who or what will be on the platform waiting for you. Indeed, tales of ambushes and firms roaming around on the tube looking for victims are legendary. Unless you are with about 20 other blokes, I would always urge you to keep yourself to yourself. Try to avoid making eye contact with anyone and if you have a funny accent (i.e. you're from outside London) I would even avoid speaking if you can.

Of course, if you are with 20 other blokes, you can be as loud and as rude as you like. Who's going to tell you off? I would, however, urge anyone using the tube to avoid the temptation of pulling the communication lever. Whilst this may well be hugely amusing on a normal train, on the tube it can be bad news. Not only will the Underground staff immediately know which carriage it was pulled in, many of the new trains have cameras in them and so they will even know who it was. In either case, they will merely move the train on to a platform and keep the doors closed until the Old Bill can come on board and pick you up. But much worse than that, if the police think anything malicious is going on they may well bring the train to a halt in a tunnel, and it will stay there until they are ready to sort you out. This, in itself, is bad enough. Because if it happens it is inevitable that in your carriage will be a woman and her kids who quickly begin screaming at full pitch as a result of claustrophobia. This will rapidly turn into a nightmare and being taken into custody by the Old Bill will come as a massive relief. Best to avoid it altogether.

Chapter Eleven

Stopping

Inevitably, as you bomb up (or down) the M1 or some other god-forsaken motorway in your car, bus or van, you will need to stop. If you are with another group of geezers, they will all know the score and you should simply follow them and do whatever they do. However, if for some reason you are on your own, you need to be careful. Stopping at a motorway service station should not be taken lightly, as, like most things involved with travel and footie, it can be very dodgy.

One of the reasons for this is historical. Back in the golden days, when coach travel began to become routine, coaches from clubs all over the country would descend on these stations, usually all at the same time. This, inevitably, led to all the hooligans causing trouble and/or removing most of the stock from the shelves of the shop by the dubious tactic of mass shop-lifting. After a time, the service-station owners became fed up with this and banned all coaches on match days. As no coach back then had toilets on board, this caused major problems for all the males, who were forced to resort to urinating in empty cans. Not the easiest thing to do as you bounce around on the back seat at 70 miles an hour.

The geezers soon wised up to this and travel in minibuses became the norm for a while, as these were exempt from the ban. However, this did not stop the fighting or the shop-lifting, and soon the Old Bill began to infest these stations to ensure everyone behaved themselves. This, in turn, led to another phenomenon: the mass footie game. These came about when hordes of geezers from all manner of clubs arrived at service stations and came under the watchful eyes of the Old Bill. For some reason, rather than indulging in fisticuffs they started to play football against each other. These games often ended up as 30-a-side affairs and were often more violent than any hooliganism would ever have been. They were a good laugh, though.

As time passed, and both football clubs and the Old Bill started to get on top of the hooligan problem at service stations, football coaches were allowed back in, but they were closely monitored and arrival and departure times were strictly enforced. This led to a steady reduction in the number of these footie games to the point where, sadly, they are rarely seen. The other consequence of all this was that the hooligans now began to use the service stations not for fighting, but to plan things or to exchange information, and this still takes place. Indeed, stop at almost any station on a Saturday and you will see groups of geezers huddled over tables, talking in whispers. These are hooligans, and you should stay away from them at all costs. Indeed, this is one of the reasons I would always advise against stopping at motorway service stations if you are travelling alone. Not only because it is incredibly sad to go to an away game by yourself, but also because a lone geezer bumping into a group of other geezers could well provide them with a bit of sport to get them in the mood.

However, for a geezer with a group of other geezers, the motorway service station is nowadays a wonderful place to be. Having set out on your journey, whoever it is with, this will almost certainly be your first break and therefore it will be the first opportunity to indulge in a bit of showing off. After all, you're flash, you're cocky and you're arrogant. You're a geezer. And you need to let everyone know that.

As you pull off the motorway into the car park, the first thing you should do is look for any signs that there are other football supporters already there. If there are, and the signs are that they are from a club other than your own, what you do next depends on what club they are from. For example, if they are from Barnet, you should be all right, but if the car park is full of Stoke City coaches, get the hell out of there. This isn't cowardice, you understand, it's merely self-preservation. Why walk into trouble if you can avoid it? However, as you're travelling in the same direction as all the other fans from your own club, the chances are that the car park will be full of club coaches bedecked in your team's colours. If this happens, then you're in. This is where the fun starts.

Having parked up, and got out of the vehicle, the first thing you should do is check your reflection in a car window. This is to ensure that everything you are wearing looks good and that you are at your best. As a geezer, your image is, after all, vital. After adopting your finest 'I am better than you' expression, stroll into the service station and casually make your way to the toilets. This should always be your first stop. Having been stuck in a car or minibus for a considerable time you will certainly need it, but you can also take the opportunity to take another good look at yourself in the mirror. Be very careful when you wash your hands here: the taps in these places are usually the push-down type and they are fierce. Splashback can cause great mirth amongst the other geezers and that is not what you need. Having washed your hands, the next port of call will be for a drink and something to eat. Most service stations now provide various fast-food outlets within their boundaries but you should never go to these. They will be full of kids and anoraks. Always go to the restaurant, as that is where all geezers go.

Walk in, go directly to the counter and ask for whatever you fancy. Never stand there looking around or start gawping at the menu, as people will think you are either a salesman or a sad. Furthermore, never complain about the prices. All prices in motorway service stations are exorbitant but remarking on them marks you out as tight. And geezers are never tight. Once you have your food and drink, you should take a table near a window to ensure that you can see all around you and then stuff your face. This is the only time you should ever start to take any notice of who or what is inside the service station with you.

As you eat, it will quickly become clear if there are any other geezers in the restaurant. They will be the ones dressed almost, but not quite, as smartly as you are. If there are, the chances are that they will be from your own club and hopefully they will recognise you or someone at your table will recognise them. If this happens, the only acknowledgement required of the other group's presence is a simple, but very visible, nod of the head. If they show no signs of recognising you and you have never seen them in your entire life, one of two things can happen. Either one of them will come over to your table and ask who you are and where you are going – in which case you should exchange pleasantries with them and wish them well on their journey – or they will simply carry on eating and totally ignore you. If this happens, it is a good thing and you should not let their presence bother you at all. Simply carry on as if they were not there and eventually one of your two groups will leave. It is as simple as that. As a novice geezer, you should never, ever even think about going over and asking anyone you do not recognise which club they are from. Not only is there the chance that they will be from your own club, in which case you will blow your own background wide open, but there is also the likelihood that they will be hooligans from another club. And they will get the right hump. With you.

This leads us nicely into the third possibility, but this one is very unpleasant – although, thankfully, it is very rare these days. If the other group have any hooligan tendencies at all and if there are more of them than there are of you, they may well start to hurl abuse at you and your group. If this happens, you are in the shit. After all, as a geezer, you cannot let anyone from another club badmouth you in front of anyone else and so all you can do is react with abuse of your own. Hopefully, if there are large numbers of other fans from your own club in the building, they will back down and leave. If not . . . well, we'll talk about hooliganism later on.

If the meal has passed by peacefully, conversation and fags should be indulged in with the other geezers at your table before making your way out to the shop. Now I can only speak from experience here. As a southerner, the joy of going up north and lording it up over the downtrodden masses is one of the great delights of being a geezer. I can only assume that it is the same for those travelling in the other direction, and I certainly hope that it is. Slagging off the bleak skylines, the power stations and the crap weather is one of the highlights of a trip to Yorkshire, as are references to *Coronation Street* (and yes, I know that's in Lancashire, but that's the point!), Arthur Scargill, whippets, and tripe and onions. In fact, every stereotypical feature known to southern man. No doubt Mike Baldwin, soft southern shites and weak beer figure just as strongly for those visiting the capital city. The visit to the motorway services' shop is the first time on the trip you will have the chance to converse with anyone from outside your own particular region and so all these references should come out. Sadly, while you and everyone else will think they are hilarious, the person behind the counter will hear them every single week and will either ignore you completely or just think you are a twat. Either way, at least you will enjoy yourself and that is all that matters. You should also take this opportunity to slag off any other fans from your own club who happen to be in the building. They are, after all, beneath you in every way, shape and form. They deserve to be ridiculed.

Eventually, the time will come to depart. After all, you have a schedule to keep to. As this time approaches, you should finish being abusive and make your purchases. Now, in the golden days, no geezer worth his salt paid for anything from a service station shop. Everything that could be smuggled out was smuggled out. Rightly or wrongly, that was the way it was, but now things have changed. These days, unless you want to suffer the ignominy of being detained by a security guard either not yet old enough to shave or too old to stand without the aid of a stick, you simply have to pay. Your purchases should, however, be limited to what you can put in your pocket. The reason for this is that it's very difficult to retain any degree of style if you are trying to carry three boxes of Mr Kipling's exceedingly good pies, a large bag of salt and vinegar crisps and two cans of Coke. If you're still that hungry, make two trips.

Then it's back on the road. Having satisfied all your needs and indulged in a bit of banter with the locals, you will be feeling both refreshed and happier. The anticipation will now start to build as you speed your way in the direction of whatever town or city awaits your arrival.

Chapter Twelve

Arriving

Arriving at your destination is another of the highlights of away travel. The buzz of anticipation will be cracking the closer you get, and the first sight of those floodlight pylons can be almost orgasmic. The closer to the actual ground you get, the stronger it feels.

This is all the better if you arrive by road, because you can first take a short detour to have a look around the ground and then, after parking up, make your way into a local public house for a few alcoholic beverages. Indeed, for those who travel by car, minibus or van, the pub is an obligatory stop and you should always allow at least an hour and a half drinking time after your arrival. Most police forces will have allocated at least one pub for the away fans and it will always have at least one or two members of the local Old Bill keeping watch. Just in case. This ensures that you can be even louder than usual and still not worry about the locals. I would not, however, recommend that you go wandering around looking for a pub unless there are a good number of you. The reason for this is that at most clubs, the pub used by the main home firm is often well away from the beaten track. Stumbling across such a place and wandering into the lounge bar to order your pint of Guinness could well be detrimental to your health. Once again, I speak from bitter experience.

If you arrive in the town by coach, then hopefully, it being a geezers' coach rather than a club one, your arrival will have been delayed by a drinking frenzy in a town or village *en route*. Therefore, you will be late enough to actually be grateful to the police for providing those two motorcyclists to facilitate your speedy movement through the traffic to the ground. Because, sadly, all coaches, including those full of anoraks run by your club, are taken directly to the ground, thanks to the police who remember only too well the past efforts of the hooligans.

If your journey was by train, stepping out of that carriage on to the platform can be a stunning experience. If the train is packed with lads and geezers, the noise will be deafening. This again is an excellent thing. It announces your arrival and lets everyone within earshot know you mean business. Inevitably, as you move along the platform you will notice that one or two members of the local constabulary will have come to greet you. Almost as inevitably, standing behind them may well be a few geezers from the home club. These geezers will be only too happy to exchange abuse with you if you want, but you should avoid this for the simple reason that the local Old Bill will blame you for any foul language they may hear and, as a result, may well decide to throw you back on the train or even in the local nick until after the game. This is not a good idea. Better to save any banter until the actual game. If you, as a geezer, want to do anything, you should merely sneer at their obviously poor clothing and lack of style. This can be done using a simple shake of the head and a wry smile.

Once they have you off the train and on the platform, the Old Bill will then decide what to do with you next, and this will depend entirely on how many of you there are. If there are a lot of you, they may decide to round you up like cattle and escort you to the ground. The route they take will be long and arduous and will also provide ample opportunity for the local geezers and wannabes to hurl both abuse and objects at you, safe in the knowledge that you cannot get anywhere near them. This is a bad thing, and escorts should be avoided at all costs. This is not as hard as it sounds, however, as most policemen are not very bright and expect all footie fans to look the same (i.e. like anoraks). Therefore you should simply hang back until they have all gone or try and bluff your way through the cordon using the pretext that you hate football and are in town to visit your mum. This is fairly easy if you are on your own or even in groups of two or three, but you may well have a problem using this reasoning if there are 30 of you, you are standing on New Street

Station in Birmingham and you come from east London. If this is the case, you should improvise.

There are, however, occasions when staying with the escort is a good idea. For example, if you are visiting a town with an exceedingly large number of geezers (i.e. Bristol), your smart clothing and obvious class will immediately highlight your presence to the local hooligans, who will be on you as soon as you escape the watchful eyes of the Old Bill. In a situation like this, all you can do is weigh up the pros and cons and make a decision on your next move based on experience and fear. However, if there is even the remotest chance that you will get a slap, I would always stay with the police.

If there are only a few of you and the locals are not much of a problem, the police will simply send you on your way. If they are nice policemen (i.e. not the West Midlands or the Met) they may even tell you which pub is marked out for the away fans. If this happens, simply make your way there, taking a taxi to save drinking time if it's a long walk. In either case, I would always avoid walking around the local town centre, as the local lads will almost certainly congregate there and unless there are a few hundred of you they will take exception to your presence. This will certainly involve you receiving abuse from them and may even mean a bit of running. This is not a good thing. Best to get to the pub and get in the swing of things with the other geezers from your club.

We have already discussed pre-match drinking but it is important to realise that drinking at away games is entirely different. It is much better. The pub you end up in will be rammed with other geezers from your club and so singing, shouting and generally being laddy is obligatory. If it's warm outside, you can even sit drinking in the pub car park, which means that you can also hurl abuse at the locals and the traffic. This is great fun. Not only that, but the local Old Bill will be in attendance and so should ensure that you are left well alone. However, much will depend upon the locals' reputation as hosts (or even your reputation as tourists), because some are down-right savage in their treatment of visitors and will think nothing of turning up and throwing things at you from across the road. After a few seasons of geezerdom, experience will tell you which towns are fine and which are not, but if you have any doubt you should merely follow the pack and you will be all right.

Once inside that pub, if you are with another group of geezers, you should never avoid buying your round. Remember the golden rule: real geezers never ponce. The only exception to this rule is food. Strangely, a geezer can do most of a day's wages on a single round but ask him to buy a bag of salt and vinegar crisps and he will get the right hump. The best way to deal with this is always to offer the money in advance if you ask someone to buy you something to eat.

Occasionally, as a geezer in a boozer in a strange town, the pub you are in will come under attack from local hooligans. When this first happens to you it is extremely frightening, but once it has happened a few times you will soon come to realise it need not be dangerous at all. I will discuss hooliganism later on, but, as a basic guide, to avoid any problems you should always avoid sitting near windows, stay away from doors and keep your back to a wall. If anything does happen, it will go off so quickly that most of the geezers will be out the door after the attacking hooligans, which will mean you will be at the back. All you need do is run towards the door, pushing people and shouting as loudly as everyone else, and no one will be any the wiser. Simple.

Chapter Thirteen

The Away Game

As match time approaches, the geezers in the pub will begin to think about moving off to the ground. This should not be done in dribs and drabs, as this can be asking for trouble from the locals. Leaving the pub should always be done *en masse*, as it is not only safer, it is also far more effective. In any case, as a geezer, these are the times you should relish, because this is what it's all about and the differences between being at home and being away are never greater than at this point. You're about to step out of a pub in a strange town and walk, in the company of other geezers, to another football ground. It's the bollocks. You're showing out and you need to let everyone know that you are there. Not by singing – the anoraks can do that – but with your style and your presence. As you walk up that road, giving it as much arrogance as you can, project yourself. Get your chest out and your head back. Dare anyone to have a pop at you. If you do it right, it will never happen. This approach, as a laxative for the home fans, should not be underestimated. And in any case, if anything does go off, the local Old Bill will be right behind you.

Another contrast between home and away games is that as a geezer you are obliged to argue with anyone who represents authority at that club. It can be either police or stewards, it doesn't matter, but unlike at home, when such people are merely an irritation, you must try and piss them off if you can. Remarks such as 'This ground is a fucking disgrace' or 'You should be paying us to come to this shit-hole' sometimes work, although you have to remember that the stewards will hear them every week and so will hardly notice them. It is not, however, a good idea to push your luck. Whilst the Old Bill will put up with so much, there is a line over which you should not tread. Do anything physical or even be critical of a policeman's parentage to his face and you may well find yourself sitting in a cell. This is not a good idea. Finding that line takes years of practice and I would advise you to leave this to others far more experienced than yourself. In any case, watching someone else give it 'the biggie' (as discussed in annex B) to the head steward is often just as humorous as doing it yourself. Primarily because if he loses the plot, you can jump in and get lairy. This will endear you to everyone else from your club. Especially the other geezers.

Before actually entering the ground, it is always worth doing a bit of loitering outside (see annex B). This will enable the other fans to see how classy your clothes are and will also let the travelling fans, and any other geezers who were in a different pub, know that you have travelled as well. This is never a bad thing. At the next home game, someone will almost certainly recognise you and acknowledge your presence.

Once inside the ground, the usual rules apply. However, the joy of away travel is that being put in one section of the ground means that all of the geezers from your club will congregate in one area. This is a good thing. Not only will you hear all of the stories of incidents during the trip up, but the noise level of the abuse directed towards the home fans will be far greater than at home because it all comes from one large group. Indeed, abuse should always be far louder and more vociferous when travelling, whilst references to the local dialect, diet or sexual preferences should be the norm. Furthermore, any gestures you use or mannerisms you adopt should always be slightly exaggerated when you are at an away game. Therefore, giving it 'the biggie' should involve far more pacing around angrily or even a bit of bobbing up and down for added effect.

Other than that, as the game progresses the usual rules apply, with just two exceptions. The first of these is if a ball comes near you during the game. At home, if this happens, you should simply duck out of the way or, if it isn't going to hit you, ignore it and then scream abuse at the ball-boys who should be doing their job and getting it back on the pitch as quickly as possible. If you are away, however, you are duty-bound to do something spectacular with the ball if you can. This can range from a vicious return header to catching the ball and then simply throwing it back to the players in one simple movement. Alternatively, if your team are winning and there are less than 30 seconds to go, you should simply kick the ball backwards into the stand as far as you can, where the other geezers will simply keep hold of it for as long as possible. This is, of course, totally pointless as the referee will simply add on the time or get another ball, but what it will do is piss off the opposing team's players and, of course, their fans. Not only that, but it will disrupt the flow of play. Not a bad thing if your boys are hanging on for dear life, and it's also tremendous fun into the bargain. Whatever you do, a simple bit of practice should be undertaken in your back garden before you try anything.

The other difference between watching a game away and watching one at home is at half-time when, if you manage to get anything to eat or drink, you are duty-bound either to take the piss out of the catering staff's accents or, if the girl behind the counter is even slightly fit, to try and pull her. This is a pointless exercise because even if you do get lucky (and you've got as much chance of winning the lottery and the pools on the same day) you can't do anything because you'd miss the second half. No bird is worth that.

While we're on the subject of pulling, I suppose it should be looked at in greater detail. I have already discussed the role of women at football (i.e. they should not have one) and, generally speaking, even thinking about pulling when you are with the other geezers at football is a no-no. The exception to this is when you travel away. If, as you tour the country, you get even the remotest sniff of a come-on from a member of the opposite sex, you must go for it. And then, if anything happens, you must tell everyone within hearing distance every single sordid detail of the liaison. If you can get her to leave wherever you found her and come with you on the coach or in the van, all the better. This is the stuff of legends, and your status amongst the other geezers will rocket.

There are, however, rules to be considered. Firstly, nothing must interfere with your enjoyment of the actual match. Missing a game because of some bit of skirt is an outrageous thing to even consider, as is actually taking her into the ground with you.

You should also realise that any trip you get her on is strictly one way. I mean, if she wants to leave Scratchwood Services and go with you to Southampton, that's great. But you certainly do not have to get her back there. That's her problem. Finally, I feel duty-bound to point out that any girl who will go on such a journey with you, no matter how stunningly good-looking or persuasive you are, is highly likely to have done the same thing with at least one or two others at some time or another in the past. Therefore, unless you have a love of doctors' waiting-rooms, always practise safe sex. A word of warning, though. If you do manage to gain any kind of carnal knowledge with a member of the opposite sex, the fact that everyone else with you will know about it means that there is a very good chance that it will find its way back to your beloved. However, worse than that, if you do go on the pull, there is also the chance that the woman you approach may blow you out. The consequences of that happening, certainly as regards any future nicknames, are dire. I guarantee it will come up in conversation on every single subsequent trip for the rest of your life.

To return to the subject of the actual game, eventually, as with all good things, it will come to an end. The result will leave you either delirious or furious, but, in any case, the time has come to leave. Or not.

Chapter Fourteen

Getting Home

As the final whistle blows, you should immediately begin moving towards the exits. Never leave your seat before this and, unlike at home games, never stop and stand to clap your team off the pitch. They will almost certainly not deserve it and will have no idea of the hardships you have suffered to get all this way to watch them play. In fact, in an ideal world, they should be clapping you out of the ground.

It is always best to stay in the company of the other geezers as you leave an away ground. This is simply to ensure that you have safety in numbers as you spill out on to the road outside. The downside to this is that you will be amongst other supporters and as you are moving towards the exits you will almost certainly hear them talking about the game you have just seen. But whereas geezers' conversations on such matters are short and to the point, other supporters, and in particular anoraks, rattle on at length and talk total and utter bollocks. For example, even though your team may have played a standard of football that would not have looked out of place during a junior school six-a-side tournament and your so-called 'striker' had yet another nightmare, someone will inevitably say 'That was a most enjoyable game' or 'I thought that Lee was very unlucky today'. Alternatively, your lads could have played out of their skins and walloped your local rivals 4–0 and your striker could have hit a 30-yard bullet, but someone is certain to say 'Well, I thought we were poor in the first half'. In either case, on hearing such drivel, your initial instinct will be to respond with a comment of your own. You must resist this impulse, because this is exactly what they are after. They want to engage you in conversation so that they can prove how knowledgeable they are about the game. That is what anoraks do. Of course, your second instinct will be to give them a slap, but, again, this should be resisted. Not only is it not nice, it may also get you arrested. Not a good idea. Get your head down, and just get out of there.

As you and the other geezers flood out into the streets, it is always worth moving across the road and indulging in a bit of loitering. This is because the local Old Bill will be in complete disarray and will have no idea which club you are from as the two sets of fans will quickly become intermingled. The other bonus here is that you may well get a close look at the local geezers. This will enable you to see what they are wearing and, if you outnumber them by a factor of ten to one, pass comment on the extremely poor quality of clothing and lack of style. This will upset them a great deal but, as you have superior numbers, they will be unable to do anything about it. If, however, they outnumber you, it is always worth making sure the other geezers from your club are close by. Just in case, you understand. I would certainly avoid responding to the comments that will inevitably come your way.

What happens next will depend on how you made your way to the ground. If you came by coach, you should get back on it and go home. Primarily because if you don't it will go without you. If you came by train, the local Old Bill will want you all gathered together before herding you in the direction of the local station. Strangely, at most clubs these days the local hooligans prefer to congregate in the train stations rather than in side streets. This is possibly because there is a very good chance that the Old Bill will concern themselves with getting you and your mates on the train first and will therefore leave them alone under the pretence that they will deal with them later on. This will simply leave them free to hurl all kinds of abuse at you in almost perfect safety. Alternatively, of course, it may be because any train station has numerous escape routes and so if things kick off they can get out quite quickly.

If you are at a train station and something happens, you should always indulge in as much abusing as possible. After all, this may well be your last chance until the next away game, so why not enjoy it? Do not worry about the police, as they will simply want you out of the town as quickly as possible and will only arrest you if you do something really stupid.

If you came by car or minibus and would like a bit more alcohol, you can always return to the pre-match pub. However, a word of warning. The post-match away pub is a very different place from the one you were in earlier. Not only will the locals be allowed back in after the game but there will almost certainly be fewer of both your lads and the local Old Bill. If you must return then be careful and tone down the abuse a bit. Better to get in your vehicle and meet up with the other geezers in another town or at a pub back in your own town. At least you can sleep on the way home and it may even be worth a return visit to the service station you stopped in on the way up.

There are, however, occasionally times when things do not happen like this and you need to know about them. Your first hint will come as you go to make your way out of the ground and notice that the Old Bill are stopping you from exiting. This is because they have decided that they are going to keep you behind for a while. Although this is a pain in the arse, it is occasionally a good thing. After all, if the team have dealt out a thrashing and the geezers (that's you) have been in the town pubs all day being mouthy and creating all kinds of problems, then the local population may be slightly unhappy. Some of them may also have decided that they would like to discuss their thoughts on your behaviour with you. You do not want this; it is a bad idea. Alternatively, depending on which club you follow and what happened in the game, the Old Bill may have decided that they want to keep you in because you are unhappy about something and may want to have a quiet word with the locals. In either case, you should complain vigorously about this to the local plods, mentioning such things as civil liberties and Members of Parliament during your ranting. It will not work, of course (I mean, what can they do? Throw you out?), but it will certainly make you feel better and will not go down too badly with your mates either.

Eventually they will decide that the time has come to let you out and will open the gates. This could be five, ten or even thirty minutes after the game has finished but by this time the Old Bill will be swarming around and the locals will all have gone. If this happens, your only viable option is to go home. The pre-match pub will be out of bounds to you and hanging around with nothing to do is very wearing. Unless you are a hooligan and have other things on your mind, there's nothing else for it but to get back home and have a few beers in your own local. There's always next week.

Part Four

The Bad Lads

Chapter 15   The Hooligans

Chapter Fifteen

The Hooligans

Much mention has already been made in this book of hooligans and the whole subject of hooliganism, and so the time has come to explain who and what these people are.

As a geezer, you will spend most of your time inside grounds trying to wind up the opposing fans. That is your mission within the scheme of things. Gestures such as 'the biggie' (see annex B), together with some of the more colourful songs you will sing every match day, are perfect for achieving this. However, even though you may occasionally ask them to 'Come on, then!', this is actually the very last thing you want. After all, if they get anywhere near you, they may actually make contact and, believe me, that can hurt. A lot. Similarly, while running around or 'lunging' (see annex B) are designed to enable you to actually hit someone else, you would never want to do it, would you? I mean, what's the point?

But for hooligans the point is that they do actually want to hit other people and they want to hurt them. Not just to damage them physically, but to hurt their reputation as well. And that's what hooliganism is all about. Reputation. The knowledge that you are a member of one of the, if not the, worst, meanest, most intimidating group of football fans in the country. It is a fiercely fought battle and the skirmishes go on week in, week out all over the country.

Hooligans are often regarded simply as thugs. People who, if they were not at football causing mayhem, would be out mugging old ladies or stealing charity collection boxes. This is bollocks. Although there are undoubtedly members of the hooligan fraternity who have very low moral standards, the majority of them are simply football fans who have taken their support for their particular club to a level that most people cannot understand. As a geezer, your love of your club should be greater than most, but if you can imagine taking it up to a level beyond even yours, then that's hooliganism. And it is the passion felt on this level that drives people on to fight for the reputation of their club. That's 'fight' as in 'violence'. This violence is itself on a number of different levels. For example, running around pushing and shoving people inside a ground is one thing, but planning ambushes on coaches or public houses miles from the stadium is something else. Yet both are done regularly and both are classed as hooliganism.

To the outsider, the whole hooliganism culture may seem like a pathetic, futile and very childish thing to be involved in, and it is. There is absolutely no point to it and there is certainly no rational reason why one person would want to physically harm another individual simply because he supports another football team. But, as we all know, football is totally irrational at any level, and every time a match is played, somewhere in that crowd will be a group of people who are looking for violence of this nature. It may be five people, it may be fifty. In the case of certain clubs facing certain fixtures, it may be two thousand or even more. Often those people will have crossed the line from geezerdom to hooligan quite by accident, getting involved in someone else's fight and coming out on top or getting away and escaping a hiding. And then, having experienced that rush of adrenalin at first hand, they have gone back for more, and then more. It becomes addictive.

The reason why they do it is a simple one. It is exciting. In fact, it is very exciting indeed. Someone – well, me, actually – recently argued that hooliganism was in fact the original extreme sport. Snow-boarding, parachuting, hang-gliding, etc., they are sports that are designed to allow the participants to experience the thrill of facing up to their fears and conquering them. But that is exactly what hooliganism is. Visiting a strange town and never knowing what is round the next corner or inside the pub you are about to enter can be a terrifying experience. As can walking out of the New Den on a Tuesday night or walking around the centre of Portsmouth two hours before kick-off. But the hooligans do it. Every single week, and the thrill they get from it never diminishes. Yet just as exciting as facing their own fears is the fact that hooliganism provides the participants with the opportunity to instil that fear in others. Chasing opposing fans through a town centre or fronting it up to a line of riot-gear-clad policemen can be astonishingly stimulating. This is where 'the buzz' comes from.

However, as a geezer, even though you may not necessarily agree with what the hooligans do, you should never, ever condemn them. You have no right to do that because their role, misguided though it is, is similar in nature to yours. They, like you, are there to belittle the opposing fans and show that you and your club are better than they are. It's the art of one-upmanship taken a few degrees further, if you like. Furthermore, most of them will have just as much style as you do and will almost certainly have graduated to hooliganism from geezerdom. This means that they will certainly know more about you than you will ever know about them. And, in any case, occasionally they can be very useful to have around.

For you, of course, this is all just background information. I mean, you wouldn't ever get involved in any of this, would you? However, make no mistake, those who do not watch our great game will certainly see you dressed up in your finest and level the accusation of hooligan directly at you. There is nothing you can do about this, as these are the people who read *The Sun* and accept every single word of it as gospel. There is no arguing with people like that. Sadly, and just as inevitably, is the fact that you, as a geezer who goes to games home and away, will at some time or another become embroiled in an incident of hooliganism. When this happens, you need to know what to do. Not only to protect yourself from any semblance of personal injury, but also to preserve your good name and reputation amongst the other geezers. There are various ways to do this but they all depend on where and when the incident happens. What you should do can only be decided at that specific moment, and that decision can only be made by you. After all, you're the one they'll be after. The only way you can make that decision is by knowing how the game works. Because hooliganism is a game and, like all games, there are rules, and within this particular diversion these rules can be very complicated. All geezers know them because they grow up with them and they are second nature. If you're going to make it out there, you need to learn them. Fast.

The first thing to realise is that anyone who walks through a turnstile has the potential to become a hooligan. It can be a geezer, like yourself, or even an anorak, and it could even be something as simple as someone spilling hot chocolate down your trousers. But if something happens and that old red mist descends, then lashing out and getting arrested will see you in court and you will be tagged by the Old Bill for ever. As a geezer, you should always be above this, of course, remaining cool, calm and aloof at all times, but occasionally it does happen, so be warned. Furthermore, although hooligans often appear to be a collection of yobs running around causing mayhem, this is sometimes not the case at all. At some clubs it is, and we'll talk about them in a while. But at some it isn't. At some clubs the hooligans are very well organised and very dangerous. These are the clubs with the worst reputations for hooliganism. I will not name them here, but suffice to say that not all the worst clubs are in the top flight.

Hooligan groups are known as 'firms' or 'crews' and will often have given themselves nicknames based on former glories or specific features of their club. For example, The 657 Crew from Portsmouth are so called because their main boys used to catch the 6.57 a.m. train every Saturday morning when Portsmouth were away. Similarly, The Chelsea Headhunters from, funnily enough, Chelsea are so called because they used to enjoy busting heads. Some nicknames, however, are beyond any comprehension. For example, there must be a reason why the hooligan firm at Bradford City are called The Ointment but it escapes me. And I can speak from experience when I tell you that The Baby Squad at Leicester City are not babies at all. Far from it, in fact.

Furthermore, some clubs, especially provincial ones, have more than one firm. Indeed, some can have upwards of five or six. They will, however, rarely fight with each other. And never when they are on their travels. That just isn't cricket. It is always worth finding out the name of the group at your own particular club, as it will inevitably come up in conversation at some point. Similarly, for obvious reasons it is always worth finding out who is 'Top Boy' at your club. He will be the most important member of the firm because he is the leader. He will be the one who plans everything and will also be the most fearless because he will be the best fighter. That is why he is known as the 'Top Boy'. He will also inevitably be on a police computer somewhere, and so to avoid joining him there it is always best to keep a distance between the two of you.

On match days, the firm or crew will always congregate in one place before the game. This is called 'mobbing up'. If they are at home this will be in their own particular public house, and if they are away they will travel mobbed up (i.e. together) and then take over a pub at their destination or even somewhere *en route*. The pub will then become the focus of the build-up to the match because it will be where everything is planned.

If a team are at home, the rules of the game state that it is up to them to repel all boarders. They have to protect their territory and defend their reputation. That is how it works. If the visiting team have no real reputation for having a hooligan following, the home firm will simply keep a wary eye on them. If the visitors have a reputation similar to the home club, the numbers will be higher and so will the expectation. The home firm will have a few scouts out and about and they will keep in touch with their own lads by mobile phone. If the visitors turn up and are spotted, the home firm may well go looking for them to indulge in fisticuffs of some kind. This is called an 'off'. They may even make contact with the visiting group and arrange to meet for a punch-up at a specific location either before or after the match. This is what is meant by a pre-arranged off.

If the visitors have a notorious hooligan following, the home fans may well decide that discretion is the better part of valour and stay in their pub, hoping that the visitors will not come looking for them. They may also hope that the local Old Bill will be aware of the situation and be all over the two groups to keep them apart. This will enable both sets of fans to indulge in a great deal of gesturing and abuse while ensuring that the police keep the peace. It's called face-saving. However, occasionally the local Old Bill will be crap and the visitors particularly nasty and they will come with the avowed intention of fighting with the home fans. This can be done in any number of ways but when it does happen it is called 'kicking it off'. For example, the visitors can contact the home fans and pre-arrange trouble themselves, or they can run down the road and chase the home fans around for a while in the hope that they will stop and fight with them. This is called 'running' and is what is meant by 'we ran them ragged'. Occasionally the visitors decide that they want to take over the pub used by the home fans to belittle the locals and show them that they are far superior individuals. For the home fans, this is a bad thing. Primarily because it means you will have to drink somewhere else.

If the visiting firm decide to do this, they can execute it in any number of ways, the more usual of which is through what is called 'the concerted attack'. This is another bad thing because not only is a pub attack a frightening thing to experience, but the landlord may well ban all footie fans for ever. If they do decide to attack the pub, the first evidence those inside will have of this is when the visiting mob turn up outside and proceed to hurl abuse at everyone inside. They will then begin to hurl objects through all the windows before bursting in and kicking the shit out of anyone inside. Alternatively, they may just appear from nowhere and run straight into the pub before anyone inside knows what is happening. This is called 'steaming' and is even more frightening than the other option. In either case, you do not want it. Therefore being in a pub that gets attacked is to be avoided at all costs. We will talk about how to do that later.

Another thing the visiting firm may well do is to indulge in a bit of 'loitering' outside the ground. This is designed to unsettle the locals, and if this happens, and if there are a good number of them, they may well do a bit of 'lunging' as well. Similarly, if they have been swarming all over your town all day unopposed, they may well walk up the road *en masse*, giving it 'the biggie' and making huge amounts of noise. This is to signal their moral victory over your pitiful support.

Inside grounds, hooliganism is, thankfully, fairly rare these days. This is in marked contrast to the golden days, when, if anything happened, it would often involve mass pitch invasions, missile throwing and even riots on the terraces. These days, gesturing and abuse hurling is usually the worst thing you will see at football. That is a very good thing indeed. Very occasionally, however, things get a little worse, and this is usually at local derbies. Indeed, with regard to derby games, most of the rules go out of the window. It matters not if you are home or away: all the hooligans will be ready for violence that, sadly, is almost inevitable at these fixtures. It is also worth noting not only that their numbers will be swelled by the return of numerous former hooligans with scores of their own to settle, but also that because of the increased stakes (local pride etc.) many of the geezers you will know will be ready for trouble. This is a bad thing, because you will be expected to be with them. After all, for all football fans, the local derby is the biggest game of the season.

The problems at these games may well involve rival supporters infiltrating the home end. This is a frequently used form of aggression because these hooligans can quickly make themselves known to the stewards, who will then drag them out across the front of the home fans, enabling them to give you all 'the biggie' as they go. Some, however, may well keep their presence quiet until their team score. At which point they will go mad in celebration and the home fans will lunge at them *en masse* until the police get them out. The irony is, of course, that, despite this lunging, few will ever actually get hit. This is because as soon as they make themselves known to all and sundry, they will already be moving towards the nearest policeman in the hope that he will protect them. Which, of course, he will. That is, after all, his job. Sadly, despite this cowardly behaviour, the presence of rival hooligans in your end will be regarded as a moral victory by the opposing fans, who will then set out to hurl abuse at you for failing to deal with them. There is no way to deal with this, and it has to go down as a defeat for the home lads. Of course, if they try it, are spotted and given the odd slap, then that's a triumph for the home supporters. But then again, at least they had the bottle to try it, which in itself is a victory of sorts. As you see, it's all very childish, but spotting interlopers is one of the biggest problems the hooligan groups face when playing at home.

In actual fact, for the hooligans, most home games are a bit of a pain, as their reputation can only be harmed by what happens. In the scheme of things there is very little to be gained by running some soft-as-shite scarfers ragged and, indeed, one of the more vigorously adhered-to unwritten rules dictates that anoraks, old gits, kids and so on are left well alone. Lads, wannabes and especially geezers are fair game, though, which is a bit of a bummer. However, occasionally reputations are enhanced at home, and when this happens, everyone celebrates. For example, if a big club comes to town and its main firm steams the local pub only to be beaten back by the locals and then given a severe spanking for their troubles, word of this will spread through the hooligan grapevine like wildfire. This will boost the reputation of the home lads immeasurably. And it happens. Not often, but occasionally. The trouble is that when it does, the next time you go up there or they visit you again they will go ballistic in an effort to redress things. This is a bad thing. In fact, it's often very bad indeed.

Of course, when the hooligan groups are not at home, it is their job to unsettle the locals when they travel. In this case, all the above positions are reversed. They have to come looking for your lads and repel them, etc. However, for the travelling hooligans, the actual journey can be just as much 'fun' as the actual games. Train stations and the London Underground can be especially dangerous places to be on match days because any number of mobs from any number of clubs can pass through there. Often at the same time. There is no rule that says your team have to be playing someone to 'kick it off' with their fans. Oh that there were, although, to be honest, most of the unwritten rules of hooliganism deal with clubs on their travels. For example, no clubs from London should ever fight with each other when outside the capital. Similarly, no clubs from outside London should fight when they are in London. There are exceptions to this, of course. For example, neither Millwall and West Ham nor Sheffield United and Sheffield Wednesday will ever be the best of mates, as their particular local rivalries run very deep indeed.

It is on away trips that most hooligan reputations are made or destroyed. Going to somewhere that has a seriously rough reputation and running a few of their lads or standing your ground and taking their main crew on toe to toe is what it's all about for the hooligans. Do that at somewhere like Bristol City and the firm's status amongst the other hooligan groups will increase markedly. Even getting a few lads into the home end is worth a shot, although to me anyone who does that deserves all the psychiatric help he obviously needs. However, on the flip side of that, if a firm have built up a decent reputation and get bladdered at somewhere like Barnet, they will be finished. Their credibility will be destroyed at a stroke.

It is also important to know that if a hooligan firm have been playing up as they make their way around their particular division, every other group in the country will very quickly know about it. This happens because the firms exchange information as they travel around the country, and mostly it takes place in pubs, at motorway service stations or, more recently, on the Internet. Eventually, however, as this firm carry on with their crusade around their respective division, they will turn up somewhere and get hammered. This hiding, when it comes, may not even be courtesy of someone from their own division. It could be anyone. But it will be administered to slap them back into line and to ensure that they realise there is always someone bigger and better than they are. And there is. There always is.

At this point, having examined why and how it occurs, I should discuss the actual act of fighting. It is, after all, the one single difference between geezerdom and hooliganism. It is important to realise, though, that most hooligans are cowards. Get them on their own and they will almost certainly be decent, friendly blokes who just want to talk football and have a laugh. In the vast majority of cases, the very last thing they will ever want to do is actually get involved in a straight one-on-one scrap. The reason for this is that being in a real fight isn't like those you see in *The Sweeney* or *Die Hard* 7; a smack in the mouth or a kick in the nether regions hurts. And it's bloody painful. Anyone who has ever had one will tell you that.

But put ten hooligans together, and they will all turn into mouthy gits who will be positively champing at the bit for the chance to have a pop at anyone. That is as long as he is on his own, because it is rare for any group of hooligans ever to set out to fight anyone unless the odds are stacked firmly in their favour. And I'm not talking two to one, I'm talking five to one at least, ten to one if possible. Furthermore, if actual physical contact takes place, it will almost certainly involve running, pushing and then running away again. An actual punch will only usually be thrown if the assailant can sink anonymously back into the crowd within half a second, and a kick is very rare indeed unless it is being used to trip someone up.

In most cases, the act of fighting at football doesn't involve fighting at all. It revolves around throwing things. Bottles, coins, bricks, ashtrays, it doesn't matter what, as long as it can be chucked. Preferably as far as possible, as this will mean that the two groups are as far apart as they can be and they will have longer to get out of the way of stuff being thrown at them. And in the vast majority of cases any act of violence between supporters at football is totally dependent on one single dominant factor: the police. Unless the hooligans concerned are deadly serious about their activities – and, rare though they are, they do exist – if the Old Bill cannot get there within 30 seconds nothing much will happen other than a great deal of gesturing and abuse hurling. This is because the sight of a single constable is as effective as Moses parting the Red Sea when it comes to driving apart two groups of yobs. Indeed, once the Old Bill turn up, it allows both groups to retreat and claim a partial victory over the other. What in footie terms is called a draw.

So, as a geezer, what is your role in all of this? Well, it's quite simple, really. Where the hooligans are, the geezers will be on the periphery. Especially when you travel away. That way, if anything kicks off the numbers are high, which is the best weapon of all. And if it does go off, the hooligans can do the running after and the geezers will stay at the back doing all the running about and making the noise. Some geezers may well even have a go themselves, but this should be avoided if at all possible. After all, it isn't very nice. But as you travel around, you will soon realise that those geezers who do have the occasional pop at someone have added status amongst their peers. You need that. If you are ever going to be a proper geezer, you have to make the other geezers believe that you can stand up for yourself if you have to. If and when you do that, your credibility will soar. The key is to achieve that without actually having to hit anyone and whilst avoiding any risk of personal injury to yourself. Although you'll be shitting yourself as it all goes off around you, it is easy. After all, I have already told you what is likely to happen. Now I'll tell you how to turn it to your advantage.

There are various ways to do this, but the best method I can think of is to utilise a number of scenarios. Before I start, however, I will tell you the five basic rules of fighting at football. Get these in your head, adapt them to the situation and you'll be home and dry and safe as houses.

The first rule of fighting at football is the most simple. Don't. If there is any way on earth to avoid any kind of violence while saving face, then take it. He who lives and runs away lives to fight another day and all that. Secondly, if two people want to have a fight, the best way to deal with it is to move one of them out of the way. Exactly the same reasoning applies if two groups want to fight, and that is the way the Old Bill deal with all football hooliganism. It really is that easy, although occasionally the groups will then turn on the police (but that is something else entirely and you never, ever want to be a part of anything like that). The third rule is just as simple. If you have distance between yourself and someone who wants to attack you, you have time. Time to think and time to act. Next, always stay cool and collected. If you can keep your head while everyone around is losing theirs then you're a better man than they are and should come out of it unscathed. Finally, and most importantly of all, nothing is worth taking a slap for.

All right, scenario one: You're in a pub and a rival fan comes in giving it 'the biggie' and offers one of your geezers out. What do you do? Simple. Having followed my earlier advice and kept as far from the doors and windows as possible, you will be on the other side of the pub from this bloke and so there is no chance that he can actually get to you. Not only that, but as you have stayed relatively sober you will be well aware of what is happening. At this point, one of three things will happen: this bloke will then proceed to hit your geezer, your geezer will hit this bloke or someone else will hit this bloke. It does not matter which it is. What you must do is start screaming 'Come on, then' and run towards the door as quickly as possible, making sure that you knock over tables or bump into everyone as you go. This will suddenly galvanise everyone else into action and they will all start screaming, shouting and generally running about getting in your way. This will slow you down sufficiently to ensure that by the time you get there it will have kicked off with all the others and you won't be able to get near to the actual participants. Either that or it will have spilled over to outside and the doors will be blocked with other geezers trying to get out. In any case, you will be a hero because everyone will have seen you go for it even though you had no chance of getting there.

What you should not do is duck into the toilets and then wait till everyone else has sorted things out. Chances are, running in there will only put you in the company of others who had the same idea. One of them will certainly grass you up as a bottler, as this will be the only way he will be able to save face.

Scenario two: You are walking down the road with another group of geezers and you suddenly notice that across the road is a rival group of supporters and they are really giving you the eye. There are two police transits 50 yards up the road and they are clearly watching you as you walk towards them. Suddenly from across the road comes a shout and they run out into the road, giving it 'the biggie'. What do you do? Simple. When this happens, your group will immediately have stopped and both groups will now be facing each other. They will also be bouncing up and down, shouting and screaming and giving it the 'Come on, then'. The one thing they will not do is cross the road, as someone might actually get hit. As soon as the police see what is happening, they will have woken up and will be moving towards you. Therefore it is only a matter of seconds before they get between the two groups. The instant a policeman enters your eyeline, you simply run out into the road almost to halfway and give it 'the biggie' yourself. The policeman will then simply thrust you back towards the pavement and you can blend back into the group. Everyone will see you do this heroic act of fearless bravery.

What you should not do is, at the first sign of trouble, run towards the policemen, screaming, 'Help me, help me!' Such an act would immediately end any aspirations of geezerdom you may have. It may also earn you a slap from the Old Bill, who will be sickened by such obvious cowardice. And quite rightly too.

Scenario three: You're inside your home ground and standing alongside the resident geezers. No one has spoken to you yet but you're not fazed by this and have remained cool. Suddenly, from down the front, a rival group of fans make themselves known and start giving it 'the biggie'. The other geezers jump up and start shouting and gesturing to register their annoyance that someone has infiltrated the home end. What should you do? Again, this is a simple one. If there are seats between you and them, there is no way that you can get to them before the stewards and Old Bill do. Therefore you should be up with the other geezers but before they move you should be off towards the front. Leading the line, as it were. If you do have the misfortune to get anywhere near one of the opposing fans before the police, simply adopt the 'Come on, then', safe in the knowledge that within milliseconds the rest of the other geezers will be next to you, the police will be on you and the opposing fans will be backing off. As you were the first away, everyone will see your performance and will inevitably be impressed.

What you should not do is follow everyone else. You have to be first. The other thing you should not do under any circumstances is actually hit anyone. This will simply invite revenge as well as trouble from the law. It's not worth it and, if you follow my advice, there isn't any need for it.

Scenario four: You're walking along the road with a group of geezers from your club. From the other direction come a rival mob who are only slightly less in number than your lot. As they walk through you, one of them says something abusive. What should you do? The best option here is, of course, to ignore it. However, bearing in mind that you need status, this isn't really an option at all. Therefore, once they are out of earshot, you should stop and say, 'Did you hear what that fucker said? Let's do the bastards!' Everyone will look at you like you are mental and tell you to leave it out. At this point you can either call the other geezers 'shitters' or simply shrug your shoulders and accept it. In either case, your bravado will not have gone unnoticed.

What you should not do is run after them yourself. They will almost certainly beat the shit out of you while your 'mates' carry on walking. You will be able to contemplate this mistake much later as you sit in casualty.

Scenario five: Similar to scenario four in every respect except that it is one of the other geezers who says 'Let's do the fuckers!'. The thing to do here is back him up. Every time. Unless the numbers are stacked firmly in your favour, the others will talk you out of it anyway, but they will be suitably impressed by your support for one of your 'mates'.

What you should not do is be the one telling them to leave it out. Unless you have status, the others will think you are a bottler. This is a bad thing.

Scenario six: You're on a train with a load of other geezers on the way to an away game. As you pull into the station and step on to the platform, you hear the screaming battle cry of 50 members of the Zulu Army who have noticed your arrival. They are currently running at full pelt towards you, preceded only by a hail of coins and bottles that they threw as they started running. What should you do? Another fairly simple one, this. Get back on the train, of course. No one said being a geezer meant getting yourself killed, did they?

What you should not do, of course, is wait for them on the platform and try to engage them in conversation. Not only will you be on your own as all the other geezers will have done the off, but the Birmingham fans will merely use you for target practice.

Scenario seven: You are in the pre-match home pub and one of the other geezers decides to take exception to the look of another supporter who keeps giving him the eye. He is clearly about to go for this bloke and you are the nearest person to him. What should you do? Easy one, this. Just watch him. The second he moves towards this other bloke, grab him and drag him away. As you do this, you must make sure that everyone is aware of what is happening by shouting at him to 'Leave it out' even though you have hold of him. You should get him right to the other side of the pub, making as much noise as possible. As you do this, you should also tell the other geezers to get the other bloke out for his own safety. Once everything has calmed down, everyone will think you are level-headed and sensible. This is a good thing.

What you should not do is jump in and thump the other bloke for him. If you do that, the chances are you'll have two of them after you, as not only have you hit someone for something that has nothing to do with you, but you have stolen someone else's thunder. He will need to extract retribution of some kind, and that means you. This will be deserved if for no other reason than that you should have remembered the golden rule: never hit anyone.

By adapting any of the previous scenarios to a given situation, you should be able to maximise the potential to improve your status amongst the other geezers. Not only that, but if you have done everything correctly, you should avoid any chance of getting a slap yourself – which is the most important thing of all.

There is, of course, another thing to consider when talking about hooliganism: the consequences. Not to those who suffer violence, although that is a terrible thing, but to yourself. After all, if you are seen to be 'involved' in a number of incidents at games home and away, the Old Bill will begin to take an interest in you. Somewhat ironically, in this instance that is actually a good thing, because as long as you do not do anything stupid, they will become a kind of guardian angel and will keep a wary eye on you. Furthermore, if the Old Bill are aware of you, the resident hooligans certainly will be as well. Indeed, they may well even ask you if you would like to join them. This, for you, is another good thing, as it will boost your standing amongst the other geezers immeasurably. You should not, however, accept their invitation. Merely tell them violence isn't your thing and that, in any case, the Old Bill are all over you. They'll love and respect you for such noble words.

Finally, on the subject of hooliganism and fighting at games, there is one thing that you should always remember. Hooliganism is serious and potentially very dangerous. Although many football fans, myself included, make light of it occasionally, it should never be condoned in any way, shape or form. It is the one single reason why football fans are segregated, why there are cameras trained on them all the time and why there are so many policemen at games these days. Not only that but, more importantly, many a decent, law-abiding football fan has been seriously hurt as a result of it and numerous individuals have lost their lives. That is a horrific thing to think about. But you should always remember it.

Part Five
Travelling Abroad

Chapter Sixteen

Over Land and Sea

Eventually, at some time in your supporting life, having integrated yourself and been accepted as a true geezer by the others at your chosen haunt, you may have the opportunity to travel abroad with your club. Obviously at some clubs such occasions will arise more regularly than at others. For example, Chelsea seem to be resident features on the European scene lately (and all power to them for that), which means that their fans will be all over the place during the season. On the other hand, with the best will in the world, Chesterfield are hardly likely to be planning a large-scale migration to a European Cup-Winners' Cup final within the next few seasons. They may, however, be planning a trip to Scandinavia for a pre-season tour. You never know. Indeed, these tours are always worth considering, as the club will usually go somewhere nice and, if you follow a smallish club, you may even get the opportunity to spend time with some of the players. This will allow you to educate them in the ways of the terrace so that they know exactly what you expect of them in the coming season. Generally speaking, though, such trips will be for one-off games, be they in cup competitions or European Champions League fixtures, and so you will be out of the country for no longer than a few days at the most, and perhaps even as little as a few hours.

Whatever the occasion, such travel is an excellent thing, and if such an opportunity presents itself to you, never turn it down. Not just because you'll have the time of your life with the other geezers, but also because you will be able to say 'I was there when we went to . . .'. This simple phrase is worth a million midweek trips to Torquay in the status stakes. You will, however, have to ensure that you are invited. This will only come about if you have done the work during the previous season and the other geezers know and accept you. It is pointless organising a trip if you are still a novice geezer, as no one will go with you and you will end up hugely out of pocket.

Apart from status, of course, the reasons why foreign travel with your club is so attractive are many and varied. Most of them are similar to the attractions of a normal away trip, of course, but leaving all your problems behind and escaping the clutches of 'er indoors for a few days rather than a few hours is clearly one of the more attractive. Personally, however, I think that these pale into insignificance behind the opportunity to act like the stereotypical English football fan abroad and abuse Johnny Foreigner for a few days. But more of that later.

However the chance presents itself, the first thing you will need to consider is transport, but as most of the opportunities for overseas travel will be within the boundaries of the European Union, this should never prove to be difficult. The club will, of course, organise trips themselves as they will want to exploit your loyalty and extort money out of you. Such trips should be avoided unless your club is going on a pre-season tour to somewhere out of the ordinary such as China or Vietnam where the people are strange and the food even stranger. In such cases, organisation is best left to those who know what they are doing.

If the team are playing somewhere 'normal' (i.e. Western Europe) then inevitably a few enterprising individuals from amongst the support will organise trips themselves. These are always worth considering, primarily because they will include time for such essentials as visits to local breweries and red-light districts. Of course, if you have managed to get in with a group of geezers and they organise a trip amongst themselves, that is the way to go. By the time you come back, you'll either be lifelong buddies or will be killing each other. How you actually get there will depend almost entirely on a combination of three factors: first, the location; second, how much time you have; and, finally, how much money you have.

If you have no time but loads of money, then fly. It is quick, easy and relatively safe. It is also very boring. You will be on the plane with hordes of affluent new-breeds who will be paying for their tickets on their corporate credit cards. They will also spend the entire flight moaning about how the food is crap and how Virgin were much better when they flew to Florida with the kids last year. If they are not doing that, they will be talking team tactics and comparing your current team to AC Milan's relegation team of 1894 or some such bollocks. You do not need any of this. Furthermore, you will be flown in shortly before the game and will be expected to fly out shortly after it. Therefore there will be no time to have a wander around the more dubious areas of the city you are visiting, nor will there be time to meet up with the other geezers and bait the locals, or to get drunk both before and after the game. Not only that, but if you do get boozed up, the airline may well refuse to fly you home. These are all bad things, but the worst aspect of flying remains the fact that it is so quick and easy. For you, the small matter of going abroad is almost irrelevant. This is just a long away trip and, after all, away trips are one of the best things about being a geezer.

Personally, if you have the time, I would always go to an away game overseas by coach. If the trip has been organised properly, there will be ample time to spend in the host city and laughs, food and, most importantly, beer will be plentiful *en route*. It will also be markedly cheaper than the plane. Not only that, but there will be someone to make sure you actually get home, and the importance of this should not be underestimated.

Of course, if you love travelling by road, you can always take the car. This is a very good option, especially if you are not driving. It gives you all the attractions of coach travel and none of the restrictions. After all, in a motor you can travel reasonably quickly and in comfort, plus you can stop wherever and when-ever you want to. You can also stay as long as you like, which is not a bad thing if you manage to pull. You should not, however, consider going in a minibus or a van. In both cases, a long journey involves uncomfortable seating, crammed accommo-dation and sweaty bodies. Three things you really do not need if you're facing a 12-hour drive to Barcelona.

To state the obvious, if you do go by road you will need to cross the Channel. With the advent of the tunnel, doing so by boat isn't obligatory any more but it should always be considered. After all, boats have bars, cafés and duty-free shops. Some even have nightclubs on board. These are attractive features if you are facing a long trip. There are, however, a few ferry operators who refuse to carry football fans on board. This outrageous slur on the character of the English supporter is a legacy from the golden days when fans often fought on board such boats. Although this very narrow-minded policy can present problems for the travelling fans, there are ways around it. For example, those enterprising lads at Millwall often hide their identity when travelling on pre-season tours by adopting pseudonyms. One of the more famous was the Bermondsey Male Voice Choir, although in recent years a coachload of members from The Combined Union of Tree Surgeons (CUNTS) have also been known to follow the south London giants on their travels.

Of course, if you have no access to a car, cannot afford to fly and have been banned from the coaches, you could always go by train. Indeed, another legacy of the Channel Tunnel is that it makes the railway a viable option, especially as most European trains are the exact opposite of the British ones. They are quick, on time, clean and relatively cheap. They also have all the same benefits of ours in that you can eat, sleep and drink as you hurtle your way towards the game in the company of loads of other geezers. The downside to European train travel is that any trip of this nature will be relatively unorganised and so it will merely be a collection of geezers with no one to care if you come home or not. You may well realise just how important this is as you languish in a German cell having got drunk and abused a member of the local Polizei. The other problem with European trains is that all the guards are power-crazed dictators who will throw you off the train at some station in the middle of nowhere without hesitation. This can be a major problem if you are drunk, do not speak the language and have no currency. And trust me when I tell you that if this happens, it is always raining.

Having decided on your method of travel, there are a few more things you need to understand before you set off. The first of these is where you will get your tickets from. Purchasing them from your club is obviously the best option. Not only is it convenient, but they will want as many people out there to support them as possible. However, as it is highly likely that tickets for Stockport County's pre-season tour of Luxembourg would almost certainly be in slightly less demand than those for a Cup-Winners' Cup semi-final involving Newcastle United and Real Madrid, this is not always an option. Indeed, in a case such as the latter when tickets are highly prized, the club may well sell out very quickly or even decide to shaft the travelling fans even more than usual. They will do this by including the ticket in a 'corporate travel' package which will also include travel and accommodation and be priced at the top end of the 'You are fucking joking' scale. It has to be said that incidents of such piracy are on the increase amongst clubs, and as it is such an affront to those who travel regularly, no true geezer would ever think about using such a scheme.

There are other ways to travel and obtain tickets and they are all outside the control of the clubs. Some of them are riskier than others, admittedly, but all are better than being a victim of greed and opportunity. The first of these, and the least risky, is simply to go out there and pay at the gate. This is, however, only really an option if the game is unlikely to be sold out, but, in any case, if you try it and it fails you can always move on to the next option, which is to use the services of a tout. This is also slightly risky, as you first have to find one and then you will have to negotiate a mutually acceptable price. However, it is worth remembering that if there are a good number of you, threats and intimidation can result in some tremendous discounts. Especially from Italians. Not that I would condone such a thing. The problem with buying from a tout, of course, is that you don't know where in the ground you will end up. Potentially this could be very dangerous, so be very careful. Of course, if you're geezers, you follow Chelsea and you have managed to buy a block of 30 tickets in the home end, then bollocks. Who cares?

Yet another option is to try and blag your way in. This is not as difficult as it may first appear, as cases of English fans going to games with tickets and returning with them unchecked are too numerous to mention. Merely flashing a colour photocopy could well be worth a go, although you would have to weigh this up against spending a few nights in a cell. You could, of course, always plead innocence and insist that you have been sold a forgery by a tout. It might work. I would not suggest bribery as an option if you are abroad unless you are fluent in the local language. The reason for this is that you do not know who or what you are talking to. Attempting to bribe an undercover police officer is one thing, but bunging some German steward 50 marks only for him to let you through a gate into the waiting arms of the local firm is something else entirely.

The final option, and by far the most risky, is to travel out and hope that the local Old Bill will simply get you into the stadium in an effort to control any potential hooliganism. Although I would definitely advise anyone against following such a course of action, it has to be said that it has proven successful on many occasions. After all, nothing is more certain to upset the locals than a large mob of geezers wandering around outside the ground with no tickets, nowhere to watch the game on television and nothing to do. Far better to have them where you can keep an eye on them. They could, of course, merely stick you all in a car park and stand guard over you. That's the risk, I'm afraid, and it's one I most certainly would not take.

If you do manage to get a ticket – or decide that instead of paying to go on some 'executive' trip you'd rather give the money to a tout – then the next thing to think about is what you should wear on your trip. Although most of the normal geezer rules apply abroad, those concerning clothes are not as important as they are when you play at home. There are a few reasons for this. The first is that your very expensive gear may well look like rags after eight hours in a hot coach, and, secondly, European football fans have absolutely no concept of style or class whatsoever. Therefore your clothes will not impress them at all. Finally, huge numbers of fans from your club – and that includes many geezers – will be wearing their replica shirts, and although it goes against the grain, there are reasons for this. Even the very thought of hordes of English football fans walking around their streets worries many Europeans. Actually seeing them in their shirts scares the shit out of them. Although a lingering legacy from the golden days, this is actually a good thing. Not only that, but wearing your shirt marks you out to the other fans from your club as you make your way across Europe, and if you support a big club with a huge travelling support this must be considered. There have been numerous cases over the years of groups from the same club fighting abroad, each thinking the other was from a different country! Who needs that? It is also worth remembering that wandering around looking for a bar in the middle of a town in Poland is made all the easier when you see one packed out with lads in your colours. I'm not trying to dissuade you from wearing your finest, perish the thought, but you need to be a little less critical of the scarfers on your travels abroad. After all, like you they will have travelled, and that takes effort and commitment. They're still scum, mind, but a bit of respect is due, however grudgingly given.

The other thing to understand as you plan your trip is that as soon as you cross that small strip of sea called the English Channel you must immediately adopt the persona of the stereotypical bigoted English bloke abroad. (I apologise to any other citizens of our great nation who may be reading this but, well, I'm English. That's what we do.) You will need to do this because everyone else does it and if you do not you will stand out like a German at a comedy club.

In these enlightened and politically correct times, it is difficult to understand exactly what this means unless you have experienced it at first hand. After all, the modern thinking is that we are all Europeans working towards a common economic and social goal, with no nation within the Union better or more important than any other. This may or may not be true (that's another debate entirely), but if it is what you believe and you are going abroad with your club, you must forget it. As a geezer abroad, your thinking will be directed by historical events, not all of which involve the great game. Indeed, as far as the English footie fans abroad, and in particular the geezers, are concerned, the English are the dog's bollocks. We are superior to everyone else because we (and it was the English Army, not the British Army) carried Europe through two World Wars until the Yanks came in and helped us out. A bit. Everyone hates us because they are not only inferior to us in every respect, they are also jealous of us and resent the fact that they weren't born here. Not only that, but if anything goes wrong they expect us to go in with the Yanks and bale them out. Just like we did in the Gulf. And let's not forget the Falklands. We had to do it all on our own because none of our European 'friends' would back us up, proving once again that they are all bastard cowards. The French were even selling the Argies bloody planes! And we invented football and won the World Cup in 1966. Their food is crap as well, and as for the beer ... And what sort of language is Dutch, for fuck's sake? Even they can't speak it properly; most of the wankers speak

English. Oh, sorry, I was getting a bit carried away there. However, you should get the general idea.

As you make your way across Europe, this type of thinking will dictate your approach to conversation with anyone who has the misfortune to meet you. At motorway service stations, in bars or on trains, anyone speaking their native tongue rather than English should be ridiculed without mercy, as should anyone who cannot understand a single word you say. Indeed, with regard to language, you should never, ever try to speak the local lingo. Not only is it a totally un-English thing to do, but all the other geezers will think you are a smart arse. When you are in shops, all prices should be converted to sterling and some of the stranger-looking coins and notes should be treated with disdain mixed with utter contempt. You must, however, be aware of the local currency and its value when you travel. There is nothing more guaranteed to make some Johnny Foreigner adopt an air of superiority than the sight of an English geezer looking totally bewildered, holding out a handful of coins so that he can take what he wants. This must be avoided.

On the subject of shopping, it is inevitable that any you do will revolve around sustenance of some kind or another. This is because most football fans travelling abroad will fuel their entire trip with beer, fags and fast food. Personally, I can't see anything wrong with this. Indeed, it is fair to say that with the possible exception of France, almost every country in Europe has fast-food outlets that are infinitely superior to much of the gunge on offer in this country. The chips in Belgium are legendary, as are the Bratwurst and Schnitzels in Germany. Despite this, it is a sad fact that most geezers abroad will simply live off burgers and Coke bought from McDonald's. This may seem odd, given the previous statement, but there is a reason for it. In Europe, they eat horses. Now, if you think about it, what is wrong with that? I mean, we eat cows, pigs, chickens, etc., so why not horses? But, for some reason, we British think it's sick. And so even the thought of it is enough to keep us out of places where ordering anything made of meat could result in a mouthful of Shergar. It's strange, it's totally irrational, but it's true.

Of course, the fact that foreigners eat horses is, for many Englishmen, a good enough reason to abuse them. As a geezer, this is a good thing, as abusing people is one of your primary functions. Therefore, locals who bear even the slightest resemblance to the stereotypical foreigner so beloved of a thousand British comedians (i.e. weaselly looking Italians with greasy hair, fat Germans with big moustaches and crap haircuts, etc.) should come in for torrents of abuse, as should older people, especially in Germany. In this case, they should be taunted with references to the last War and the bombing of the East End. Similarly, wherever you are in Europe, songs about Winston Churchill, two World Wars and one World Cup, etc., should also proliferate. The only exception to this will be if you need to deal with customs officials or border guards. Indeed, if you have to deal with any kind of officialdom, you need to be cool, calm and, above all, respectful. The powers these people have are immense and they are only too happy to use them if it means pissing off a few Englishmen. They can keep you there for days, strip you and your car and confiscate it if they find anything. Be nice, be legal and they'll be fine. You can always abuse them once you leave them behind.

The one type of officialdom you will definitely come up against during your trip is the Old Bill. Indeed, I guarantee that when you finally arrive at the town or city hosting your particular game, they will be there waiting for you. Not the good old British bobby, either, but men with guns, big sticks and no sense of humour. It would be easy to say that most police forces throughout Europe are decent blokes, and I am sure that when nothing much is happening they are. But during every single second of your stay, the exact opposite is true. The merest sight of an English football fan turns all foreign policemen into complete bastards. During the build-up to the game in question, they will have been force-fed images of English football fans causing mayhem back in the '70s and will firmly believe that every English football supporter is a full-bore and hard-core hooligan. They will, therefore, think that World War III is about to descend on them and it is their job to ensure that you behave yourselves and do not cause the locals too many problems. Trust me when I tell you that they will not really be too concerned how they achieve that. Those sticks they carry are hard. And they hurt. The thought of cracking a few heads with one, especially English heads, fills many of them with glee. You should not, therefore, give them the chance.

You should not, however, adopt a submissive approach to your role. You are there to represent your club and then your country.

You, as a geezer, need to let everyone know that you have arrived. You just need to make sure that you do it in safety. And there are ways to do that.

The first thing that will happen as soon as you arrive is that the travelling fans will mob up. They will do this in small bars, at the train station or in the town square. This is for protection. Not from the locals, who we will discuss in a moment, but from the Old Bill. There is safety in numbers and even the most rabid Italian copper will be loath to get stroppy if there are 300 lads in close proximity. Once this has begun to take place, these mobs will then move around until they find a few large bars they can take over. Ideally, the Old Bill will have thought of this and set aside a few streets where you will be able to congregate while they keep the locals away. If this happens, your time during the build-up to the game will be excellent. Those streets will become a little corner of England and the beer, food and singing will flow freely. If they haven't made any such provision, they will simply follow you around, pissing you off until kick-off time.

Eventually, as you hang around for the game, you may well come into contact with a few of the local lads. You should never be concerned about this. As a geezer with your club you are already superior to everyone else, but any local football fan abroad is inferior even to an armchair. They don't even have the saving grace of being English to boost their personal profile. Make no mistake, every foreign football fan is scared shitless of the British supporters and will therefore treat you with the utmost respect. This is the one redeeming feature of the problems associated with the golden days. They look up to us as the ultimate in football support. They copy our clothes, songs and nicknames. They do not, however, have the British class and style that has evolved over centuries. Sadly, some of them copy our hooligans as well and occasionally problems will occur with the locals that require sorting out. This is not your problem. Your own hooligans can do that and they will be only too happy to do so. However, it is inevitable that if it does kick off, the local Old Bill will treat everyone as a hooligan and if they get hold of you will batter you senseless. It is therefore better to distance yourself from all of this if you can. However, if you can't, and conflict is unavoidable, it is better to be within sight of your club's main lads, as they will be only too ready to help you out.

Now, there is a golden rule that all English football fans adhere to when they are abroad. It is simply that the English run from no one. The numbers involved are irrelevant. Some even believe that it is better to take a kicking than to run from Johnny Foreigner, but personally I think this is bollocks. However, as a geezer in a foreign land, once you know this you must always stand your ground if you get caught up in anything. The Old Bill will not come to your aid. In fact they will blame you because you're English and in their country, so you must front up those who wish to cause you harm. Usually the fact that you stand will scare the shit out of them anyway and they will back off and then run away. No bottle, you see. However, if it gets serious, simply blend into the crowd once the Old Bill steam in and avoid doing anything that could get you either hurt or nicked.

Hopefully, though, nothing naughty will happen before the game, and so after a few beers with the other geezers you should simply follow the pack and get to the ground. I would always advise anyone watching a game abroad to go directly into the stadium once they get there. The reason for this is that many grounds abroad will have put in place all kinds of security to deal with any hooligans and they will also want to piss the English fans off a bit. Therefore it could take ages to get in, meaning that if you leave it late you might miss some of the game. After coming all that way is it really worth the risk? In any case, the locals always seem to get in to games really early abroad, so what's the point in staying outside? As you make your way in, simply do what everyone else does to avoid drawing attention to yourself. That means no abusing, no singing and no gesturing. That way you'll get in with the minimum of fuss.

Having made your way into the ground, you will soon come across people you should recognise from your club. Nothing gives you a better feeling than bumping into a bloke you hardly know when you're inside a ground in a foreign land. He will welcome you like a long-lost brother and, if he's a geezer, you should respond accordingly. If he's an anorak and you're with the other geezers, merely nod in his direction.

Inside the ground, the normal rules of football fandom apply. However, when you are abroad the team should respond far better to your support as even they will appreciate the fact that you have travelled so far to see them play. With this in mind, you should not hurl abuse at your own players when you are overseas. If they play crap, simply grin and bear it. The other group you should not abuse inside grounds abroad are the Old Bill. They will simply throw you out, beat the shit out of you or maybe even both. In any case, these are not attractive options.

Once the game finishes and the police finally let you out of the ground, you should simply return to the bars from whence you came and get wrecked. Depending on the result, the locals may well be unhappy with this, but you should not worry about them. Safety in numbers, and all that. Of course, if you are unhappy with the result, they will be delirious and will give you loads of verbal. This should be ignored. You, after all, are British. Gloating is not a part of your nature and so you should be disgusted by those who sink to such a level. However, if it starts to get on your nerves, simply start singing song after song after song. The locals will have no idea what is going on and in the end will simply shut up and go home.

At this stage, with the game over, the lager flowing and your return journey imminent, trouble may well break out as alcohol and xenophobia begin to influence the behaviour of everyone. Especially the geezers and the hooligans. In my experience of such matters, if this happens it inevitably involves a degree of provocation from the Old Bill, as they will be desperate to prove to the locals that their presence was necessary and that they did a good job. They will strut around giving it the large one and will be desperate to arrest or batter anyone who steps out of line. Do not do anything to attract attention and you will be fine.

Finally the time will come to leave and come home. Your journey should simply be a repeat of the trip out but should also be enhanced by your experiences and, with luck, a good result. As you wend your way across Europe with a load of other geezers, fresh from watching your lads in action, be it the European Cup final or a mickey mouse pre-season tournament in Sweden, you should take time out to reflect on a simple fact: you've arrived, mate. Trips of this nature are what you'll be talking about in the end-of-season pubs, not just this season but in seasons to come. You made the effort and you were there. This is what it's all about. You made it. Now you can finally call yourself a geezer.

Chapter Seventeen

The National Sides

If you support a club who frequently make excursions into Europe, trips abroad will soon become second nature to you. If this is the case then good luck to you, but, let's be honest, not everyone will have the chance to watch their side play in any kind of competition abroad on a regular basis. And, let's face it, even the idea of going on a pre-season tour has me lapsing into a coma no matter where the team are going. But if you yearn to travel and watch football with some kind of meaning and relevance, there is, of course, another option. That is to travel abroad with the national side. I cannot stress forcibly enough that this is always a very good idea indeed. Not only will you have all of the attractions of travel we have already discussed, but you will also have an added, and very appealing, bonus. When England make their way overseas, very few, if any, old gits, kids or women will travel. There are a number of reasons for this, the main one being that most internationals are played in midweek. However, the England following also has something of a reputation preceding it which does deter some less passionate supporters from undertaking any journey to support them. We will look at this in a little while. What this actually means in real terms, of course, is that the vast majority of supporters who go will be male. Either geezers, lads or sads, together with the odd hooligan. As you will agree, this is a top mix.

However, before we get on to the good points, you must be aware of the fact that there are a few essential differences between

following club and country, and you, as a geezer, really do need
to understand what these are.

The first thing you must do is forget the media-fed idea that
the national side is vital to the success of the game and that we,
as true football fans, should all be passionate about England. This
is bollocks. As a geezer, your club should be the most important
thing in your footballing life, coming before all else. Therefore, it
follows that the national side must always be placed strictly
second in your footballing affections. This is the same if you are
Scottish, Welsh or Irish. If you cannot grasp that, ask yourself this
question. Given the choice, which is the more important to you:
England winning the European Championships or your lads
winning on any single Saturday of the coming season? If you are
a true geezer, the answer will be obvious. Personally, as a fan of a
lower-division club, I do not care about the national side at all
because I do not feel they are a true representation of the English
game. That's my opinion, and as I am a stubborn bastard, it is
unlikely ever to change. I also have severe problems with the
management, the players and, especially, Wembley Stadium. In
fact, even the concept of a 'national' team seems odd and
outdated to me. What's the point of it? It can't be to prove our
game is the best – we know that already – but in the Premier
League most of the quality football comes from the legions of
foreign imports who obviously aren't available to the national
side. I could go on, of course, for ages, but I accept that not
everyone shares my views on this subject, and as I am supposed
to be guiding you through the minefield that is geezerdom, I will
continue.

The one thing that the national side does do that is of
immense value to all football fans, not just the geezers, is to
provide a diversion from the domestic game. This is vital if you
support a shit club and you are having a torrid time of it. Such
as Spurs. If you and your club are in this category, an England
fixture is a bloody relief. It gives you something else to concentrate on for at least 90 minutes, and the importance of that
cannot be understated.

You should never, however, contemplate watching England in
the flesh if you have to part with money to get into Wembley. It
is not only a toilet of a ground, it is also very expensive to enter
and for most games the majority of the crowd will consist of kids

and corporate clients. All of them will have acquired either free or very cheap tickets and none of them will have the remotest concept of how to create any kind of atmosphere. Indeed, as far as I am concerned, if you are looking for everything that is wrong with the game in this country then go to Wembley for any England friendly. It is the domain of face-painted families and anoraks who were sucked into the black hole that is football commercialism during Euro '96. As far as England at home is concerned, your money is best spent in the pub with the other geezers. Indeed, the one true value of satellite television is that it shows all of the internationals live, and all football fans learnt long ago that the greatest invention of the twentieth century is the big-screen TV.

No, if you – or anyone else, for that matter – want to find the true spirit of England and the English support, you need to travel away with the national side because that is a different thing entirely.

The first thing to realise is that while you, as a geezer, will always travel to watch your club if you can, England are only worth following if the game has any degree of importance. That means qualifiers or proper tournaments such as the World Cup or the European Championships. Nothing else. After all, what's the point in travelling all the way to somewhere like Morocco for a 'friendly' game that has no real meaning? Exactly. The only people to undertake such a trip will be anoraks or people with more money than sense. This will be proven by the fact that they almost inevitably fly to such games, and we all know what that means.

It is also worth noting that when you watch the national side abroad, your dislike of a particular player should be put to one side and everyone wearing the shirt given your total support. Never mind the fact that you are Everton till the day you die, if young Robbie Fowler and Michael Owen are out there doing the business, you should be 110 per cent behind them. They, like you, are representing the country, not their club. On a similar note, when you travel abroad, all inter-club hostilities should be put aside. Not rivalries, but hostilities. After all, with the best will in the world, I, as a Watford fan, would not piss on a L*t*n T*wn fan if he were on fire. Being at the World Cup finals in France isn't going to change that one iota. But being out there does mean that I shouldn't begin hurling abuse at him at the first sight of their ridiculous shirt. I probably would, mind, but I shouldn't. In any case, the wearing of club colours when abroad with England should always be discouraged for that very reason. Even the hooligans seem to accept the concept of neutrality, and we will discuss them and their activities in a moment.

Most important of all, however, is that whilst English sides coming to town are cause for concern amongst citizens and Old Bill alike, the national side turning up is something else entirely. The image of the stereotypical England fan which grew out of the golden days has changed little over the years and we are still regarded by all and sundry as the worst-behaved supporters there are. The fact that this isn't the case at all seems to have escaped the entire Western world, and so when England come to town, the locals will go into siege mode and the Old Bill will bring out enough weaponry to arm a small African nation. This, of course, merely causes more problems than it solves. The unwritten rule that 'England run from no one' ensures that any sort of confrontation will end in trouble of some kind or another, as the local Old Bill will demand that the English lads back down. Sadly, such stand-offs have all too often ended in violence and serious injuries.

For the hooligans, this is food and drink. They relish the thought of playing up abroad with England as they see their role in this context as defending the honour of the country. Misguided as this is, it is the one single reason why, as with the geezers, the hooligans will put many, but not all, of their rivalries aside for England trips abroad. Indeed, the Old Bill in England have often said that the hooligan firms will even join together to form so-called 'super-firms' for big games. Whilst in actual fact this is total bollocks, the fact that a fair few firms will travel to England games together is enough of a reason for them to be concerned. The other big plus for the hooligans is that being seen by the local Old Bill as an invasion force means that they can more or less dictate proceedings. This is because all the other fans, geezers included, know full well that if or when it kicks off, the hooligans will be the only ones able to protect them. That may seem slightly perverse, but it is totally true. After all, if someone else wants to wade in and take the flak then let them. That's what I say. The consequence of this is that when you travel abroad with England, no matter what your role amongst the fans, you are perceived as being a certain kind of animal. You are all guilty by association. For the individual, this is where the problems start, and so you should be aware of what may take place.

As you should know by now, being drunk and abusive is part and parcel of being a football fan, especially a geezer. However, behaving like that at home is one thing; doing it abroad is another and doing it abroad with England something else entirely. The reasons for this are simple. Because of the concentration of geezers from all over the country, not only are there far more people hurling that abuse, but the degree and nature of it is heightened by the addition of a new factor when you are supporting England as opposed to your club side: xenophobia. Normally, I would never support such a concept as this, as I would much rather advocate patriotism. For me, loving my own country is infinitely preferable to hating everyone else's. However, rightly or wrongly, a geezer by his very nature has to think that he is the dog's bollocks and that everyone outside his immediate circle is inferior to him. This translates quite easily into a dislike of other supporters, other clubs and therefore other countries. The perfect description of xenophobia, in fact. The press, having seized on this in the past and, surprise surprise, got it all wrong, have, as a result, labelled all England fans as right-wing thugs and this tag has stuck for a number of years now. When you throw in the fact that supporting England abroad means that you support the team under our national flag, you have got real problems on the image front. After all, the cross of St George is the one single symbol guaranteed to send any politically correct, middle-class do-gooder into a major-league rage. Somewhat perversely, England fans, and especially the geezers and the hooligans, have traditionally played up to this when abroad, primarily because it scares the shit out of the locals. If you are going to travel with England on a regular basis, you need to be prepared to handle being stuck with this image for a while. After all, it isn't very nice.

Travelling with England, however, is not all doom and gloom. Far from it. Not only will you bump into groups of other English football fans as you travel, but as you pour into a town or city in some strange country, the feeling that the English are taking the place over can be astonishingly exhilarating. If you are going for a tournament, all the better, because you could be there for weeks on end and the bars and cafés will soon be like second homes. Furthermore, whilst being abroad with your mates is top notch, being abroad and spending time in the company of other geezers away from the pressures of the domestic game can be a very rewarding experience. Lifelong friendships are frequently formed with people you would never normally meet, as you and your mates spend hour after hour recounting all the stories that you are bored shitless with. The fact that this normally happens in bars probably helps.

It is also worth noting that not all host countries will be against your presence. Some will actually adopt a guarded welcome, and as long as everyone behaves themselves the whole experience will be superb. The bar owners will be friendly, the food excellent and, if you're lucky, the women willing. What more can you possibly ask? Even the games can be better. Indeed, the thrill of watching England win away can be like nothing else you will ever experience. It really can. Conversely, watching England get dicked by some Third World country such as Turkey (no offence meant) can be a soul-destroying ordeal. Especially if you've travelled for days to get there and have been getting grief from the local Old Bill since the moment you arrived. When you go abroad, be it with your club or with your country, that's the chance you take. But once you've done it, I guarantee you'll want to do it again.

At this point, I should offer up an apology because I have only talked about England. I should apologise, but I won't. You see, the reason I have written about England and being abroad with the national side is because they are *my* national side. I have not mentioned Scotland, Wales or Ireland in this section of the book because I have no experience of being abroad with any of them and, to be perfectly honest, I would not want any. I am, however, well aware that these three nations are perceived entirely differently from the England supporters when they travel, and good luck to them for that. I wish with all of my heart that the English fans could travel and be welcomed in the same way as the Scots, Welsh and Irish are. Instead we are treated like an invading army, and that is entirely due to our history of hooliganism. Sadly, we will have to live with that for some time yet. However, if you take out the references to hooliganism, most of the things I have said here apply equally to the other nations of the union. Travelling with your country is a rewarding and fulfilling experience. Do it when you can, because, both as a male and as a geezer, your supporting life will be enriched by the experience.

Part Six

Warning!

Chapter Eighteen

The Drawbacks

So far, this entire book has been about the great and good things associated with a life of geezerdom. The fact that it has taken me this long to impart even a fraction of my immense knowledge is testimony to the fact that setting out on this path is one of the greatest things you will ever do. It will certainly be amongst the most enjoyable. However, I must now take the time to warn you that a lifetime of geezerdom is not all sweetness and light. There are a few drawbacks associated with this lifestyle, and although it may well be too late by now, it is only fair that I let you know what is in store for you.

All football fans know that supporting a club quickly turns into an obsession. It is not, as I have said, about 22 men kicking a ball around for 90 minutes. It is more than that. For most football supporters, as this is a lifelong link, the things that accompany their patronage will have been absorbed into their psyche from a young age. They will be second nature to them and, therefore, done as a matter of course (for example planning holidays around the fixture list, naming children after players, etc.). As a relative newcomer, you will have to learn all of this, and as you do that, you will become aware that your approach to the game itself will change.

Initially, you will begin to notice that your daily newspaper takes on added significance. Whereas you have previously digested the news and current affairs and then taken cursory glances at the back pages, this will be reversed. The back pages will become all-important, and eventually you hardly bother with the rest. Inevitably, you will realise that your daily paper is no longer sufficient to satisfy your hunger for information and gossip on the great game. This will be sooner rather than later if you support a team from outside the Premiership as, judging by the lack of coverage in most tabloids, many of them seem to believe that football doesn't exist outside the top flight.

Having realised this, you will then start to buy the odd magazine and a couple of Sundays, rather than just your usual *News of the World*. Although this will keep you going for a while, your desire for news of the great game will eventually outstrip even this amount of newsprint and you will move on to the next phase of the obsession. Without thinking, you'll end up standing in the newsagent's for hours on end reading every paper and football magazine that comes out. When you become aware that you are doing this, do not be alarmed. It is perfectly normal, and if you look around you you will see numerous others doing exactly the same thing. The fact that this takes place has now begun to filter through to the editors of various football magazines, who have taken action to stamp it out and sell more copies. This has been done by the simple ruse of shrink-wrapping them, which means that you cannot read what's inside without buying a copy. This is outrageous and potentially life-threatening. It is certainly bank-balance-threatening, as you will then have to start buying them.

Once you reach this stage, your desire for information will begin to outstrip even the amount provided by the tabloids and the monthly glossies. A teletext television will then become a vital, must-have accessory. Once this is installed in your front room, a battle of wills will commence. Initially, you'll only look at it at lunchtime and in the evening, but as its pull on you increases, you'll end up surveying it at least once every hour to keep abreast of developments. If a game is in progress, especially if it's relevant to your lads and their position in your division, the score will be checked at least once per minute.

Eventually, even this will not be enough to satisfy your hunger and you will start calling the dreaded 0898 club-call numbers to get the latest gossip on your lads. If you can, you will even get on the Internet to surf every footballing website known to man, and you may even end up spending time 'talking' to like-minded saddos on the bulletin pages. In the end, the only time you're not reading a paper, waiting for the teletext page to turn over or surfing the net is when you're on your way to a game. And even then you'll have a magazine in your pocket and the club-call number dialled into your mobile.

These are just a few of the consequences of being a bloke who likes football and they are unavoidable. However, for you, as a geezer, supporting your club means much, much more than that. The reason for this is a simple one. You see, all geezers, no matter what club they support, have one distinctive quality that sets them apart from every other type of football fan. It isn't just the obsession with their clothes, their air of superiority or even their tendency to hurl abuse, it's the fact that they are arrogant.

Being arrogant, especially in the context of being a geezer, means that you dislike and distrust everyone outside your immediate circle. This is because, as far as you are concerned, they are inferior to you. Now, in my vast experience of such things, it is impossible to be arrogant on a part-time basis. Therefore, once you begin to adopt this characteristic as a feature of your persona as a geezer, it will eventually filter through to your 'normal' everyday existence. There is no way of avoiding this, I'm afraid, as it is predetermined, but, to be honest, if you're going to be a true geezer it is also essential. After all, if you're going to do it properly, you have to live the life. You can't just be a geezer on match days. It doesn't work like that. It takes you over.

The first time you become aware of this will almost certainly be when you go shopping. You will suddenly realise that everything you look at begins to relate to your love of the game. Or, to be more specific, your club. Given the massive pulling power the commercial world has exerted over the game in recent years, this should not really surprise you. After all, sponsors spend millions to get their names plastered across the front of football shirts. This isn't just out of generosity, it's in an effort to get the general public to buy their products. Such has been the effect of this commercialism on our great game that these sponsors and the clubs they fund frequently blend into one entity rather than remaining two distinct ones. This is especially significant to you. As a geezer, with your inherent dislike and distrust of everyone else, a club and its sponsor become inseparable and your money will therefore be spent accordingly. For example, no Leeds United fan in their right mind would buy any Sharp product because of their long-term sponsorship of Manchester United. Nor would they drink Carlsberg Lager (Liverpool), eat a bag of Walkers crisps (Leicester City) or use a Hewlett Packard computer (Spurs). Similarly, I, together with many of the other geezers who frequent Vicarage Road, would never buy a Vauxhall in a million years because of their links with Scum Town, not just as a former sponsor but also as that town's major employer. And yes, by that I do mean that I would gain a perverse kind of pleasure from all L*t*n T*wn supporters being unemployed and suffering. Guilt by association, you see.

Your role as a geezer, and therefore as the guardian of your chosen club's reputation and honour, will also ensure that trips out shopping will begin to hold additional interest. As you stroll around, your eyes will scan the masses for even the merest sight of a replica shirt from any club other than yours. When you spot one, it will necessitate at least some kind of sneer and may even require an abusive remark of some kind. If it is a local rival, a simple laugh and a shake of the head can be very effective, although a scathing comment is infinitely preferable. It will certainly make you feel better. It should also be mentioned that the sight of your club's colours in the local town centre, be it on the back of some middle-aged anorak or that of a ten-year-old kid, will inevitably send a warm glow of satisfaction coursing through the veins. Especially if you support a lower-division club.

However, the influences that the game exerts on you will not simply end on walking around shopping malls or the purchasing of consumer items. Far from it. As the obsession takes over, your home will become a shrine to your support. The interior decoration will inevitably be influenced by your club colours at some time or another, as will your garden if you can manage it (supporting a club who play in yellow and red makes laying out the flower beds an easy task but I have often wondered how Newcastle United fans manage). Eventually, as the shrine turns into a fortress, you will begin to quiz workmen who come to your home about their own particular footballing allegiance before they are allowed entry. If they support a club you do not like, especially if they follow a local rival, you will simply refuse them entry and hire someone else. Even if they make it over the front step, you will watch them like a hawk and eject them if you hear anything resembling a mocking reference to your club or anyone associated with it. Of course, if they support the same club as you, they will be welcomed with open arms no matter what the quality of their work.

Your family life will not be immune to this either. If you are single, your conversation will revolve around the great game and you will quickly learn to avoid like the proverbial plague any woman who tells you she likes football. Not just because all geezers know full well that women and football do not mix, but also because if you actually start up a relationship, you may be desperate for a bout of horizontal wrestling one night and promise to take her to a game in return for 'favours'. After all, we're all human. In the cold light of day, she may well hold you to your word and no bird is worth such a risk. If you do actually manage to find a girl who hates football but absolutely accepts your love for it, understands the fact that she will always remain second to it in your heart and realises that you will go to every single game, you will marry her. No matter what she looks like. And the wedding will be in the close season so that the other geezers can attend. (Yes, I know such girls are hard to find, but they are out there, and once you have one, keep hold of her, for God's sake.)

When you eventually have children, anything less than a son will be deemed a failure and you will immediately convince your wife that you should try again. When you do finally succeed, your desire to name your newborn son after the entire first-team squad will be frightening, although you will resist it and settle for registering him as a member of the junior supporters' club by phone from the delivery room. As he grows, he will be photographed in babygros with such messages as 'I'm the best dribbler at Watford' embroidered on the front and his bedroom will be plastered in posters of the team to indoctrinate him into the ways of your club. You will then take him to a few home games early on in his life to ensure that the bug bites and he follows in your footsteps.

If you have daughters, they will be discouraged from liking football at every turn. This will be done by constantly singing and chanting about your beloved club at all hours of the day and night and going into horrific sulks every time your team loses. They will be further brainwashed into associating football with pain and disappointment by you walking into the front room and putting on the teletext right in the middle of their favourite television programmes or making them miss them altogether if there is a game on the other side. Having indoctrinated them in this way during their early years, as they reach their early teens you will give them money every Saturday to go shopping. This will finally deter them from even thinking about asking to go to a game with you.

As they grow older, you will make it clear to them in no uncertain terms that any boys they even contemplate bringing home to meet you should support the same club as you do – which is somewhat ironic, as the very last type of person you would want your daughter to go out with is a geezer. When they do eventually bring someone home, he will be quizzed at great length about his and his entire family's support before he is accepted in any way, shape or form. If there are any doubts at all, you will simply throw him out and warn him off. I know you will do all this, of course, because I do it.

If you are already married, your new-found obsession will eventually wear down even the most anti-footballing wife and she will be only too glad to see the back of you every match day. You should remember, though, if this applies to you that your wife will have known you before you even discovered football, never mind turned into a geezer. Therefore, she may not give up without a fight and may well pull a few stunts of her own in an effort to get you back on track. You should be ready for these.

One of the favourites is to tell you that you must give her exactly the same amount of money to spend on clothes as you spend on going to football. There is no point arguing this one, so simply bite the bullet and cough up. However, the amount you give her should bear absolutely no relationship to what you actually spend following your lads. Primarily because if she ever found out what your love affair with the great game was actually costing, she would go mental. Another favoured tactic amongst football widows is to try and make you feel guilty every time you walk out of the door. This will be done by staring out of the window at you as you drive off with an expression of dismay etched across her face to signify the fact that you are abandoning her and your children (if you have any). However, this is doomed to failure as no true geezer ever feels guilty about anything, and nor should he. The problem here is that women do not understand this concept at all and so if it happens to you your wife will simply have the hump with you for a few days after each and every game. She will abandon this tactic in the end, though. I promise. It may take a few seasons, mind.

Inevitably, the time will come when something is arranged on a match day and your wife will want to go. With you. It may be, for example, a wedding. You are therefore faced with a stark choice – or, rather, you're not. What you have to do is convince your wife that you will get there when you can. I cannot guide you here, as not only do I not know your wife (if you have one) and how she would react to such a situation, but, to be honest, I've hardly managed to sort this one out with my own!

Marriage is, however, dependent on give and take, and so there will be times when you simply have to bite the bullet and accept your fate. For example, when your first son is born, even though you will be desperate to name him after every single player in that year's squad, she may not be totally convinced. In this case, you should be prepared to concede defeat. You can always give the lad a nickname later on.

Just as the obsession bites at home, it will also hit your place of work. If you are lucky enough to work with loads of men who support the same club as you, Mondays will turn into a lengthy post-mortem of the previous game and, as a geezer, your own activities will be discussed at great length. After all, many of the older men will have once been geezers themselves and will want to know what's going on.

If, however, you work with loads of blokes who support other clubs, the workplace turns into a battleground. A battle of wills and wits, that is. If this is the case, then work simply becomes an extension of the terrace. Somewhere for you to wind up opposing fans and score points off them. This can be done in numerous ways, ranging from abusive screen-savers in your club colours to spitting in their tea. In any case, such pranks demand a great deal of inventiveness and should be shared only when you are in the pre-match pub with other like-minded individuals who understand totally the problems such a situation brings. If you are lucky enough to have the added bonus of being in charge of people who are foolish enough to support a different club from you, especially if it's a local rival, you will end up sending them on every shit job you can find. It will not only make them suffer, it will make you feel much better. Especially if your club are not doing so well. If, however, you work for someone who supports your local rivals, knowing that you, as a geezer, are totally committed to your club will mean that he will make your life hell. And then you will quit. But only after doing something absolutely horrific to get one over on him. This can be as delightful (for you, anyway) as shitting in the tea urn or filling his coffee pot with laxative, but, whatever you do, you must tell him as you walk out the door for the last time. And no geezer worth his salt takes a job that could possibly involve him working on match days. If you have one of these already, resign.

Whilst most of the consequences associated with a life of football fandom listed above could apply equally to any type of football fan (with the obvious exception of armchairs), as a geezer there are a number of others that apply specifically to you. Sadly, they all revolve around attending games. You see, adopting a life of geezerdom is not all lager and labels. With it come responsibilities. Not only to your club, but to your mates.

Initially, being a newcomer to geezerdom, your appearance at home games will be sufficient. After all, you are working your way into a culture that, for those already there, has been a way of life for many years. However, once your appearance at away games starts to be noticed, and certainly once you start going with other geezers, there is no going back. You will have to attend every single away fixture. On the face of it, this is a bonus, and for the vast majority of the time it will be. However, the time will eventually come when you simply do not fancy going and need a break. After all, if you work hard all week and the hours are long, you may well be shagged out by Saturday and after a season of crap games and long trips you may just want to stay in bed. This, on the face of it, is perfectly understandable. The problem is, as you spend time with other geezers and observe what goes on, you will soon come to realise that there are very few excuses that are powerful enough to explain or justify your absence from any game. It's snowing outside, being hungover, being on a promise or fancying a lie-in are simply not good enough. Neither, for that matter, is being skint. After all, if you're a true geezer, you will always have money in your pocket, but if you are really desperate, one of the other geezers will always lend you the cash. He will do that because if he were skint, you would lend it to him. That is what geezers do. And all geezers settle their debts to each other. Without question. That's the law. Of course, there are excuses that are powerful enough to keep you away but usually these involve either illness or death. And even then that only applies to you or, if you have one, your immediate family. Mums, dads, aunties, grannies – none of them count. You must accept this and, if you have one, so must your family. Of course, if your dad was once a geezer he will understand perfectly.

The other problem about being a geezer is a personal one. It may or may not apply to you but for me it is one of the great drawbacks of geezerdom. You see, much as I love travelling around in the company of other geezers, as a southerner, I hate going up north. Every time I go there it's either raining, snowing, freezing cold, dark, miserable or bleak. Or even all of them put together. The women all look ropy, the blokes look rough and the accents are all comic. I hate the sight of the pit heads, slag heaps and power stations that seem to be a feature of every northern town I have ever visited, and I have to grit my teeth every time I see a cobbled street. All the clubs have stupid names like Wigan Athletic or Preston North End and the geezers dress about ten years behind us trend-setters in the south. Manchester, which according to everyone who lives in it is the centre of the entire music and fashion world, is in fact a toilet (and if it's so great, why do all the professional Mancunians live in London?). And as for Liverpool . . . well, let's just say I like my car with wheels, thanks. Geordies are all mad and speak in an alien tongue I have never been able to understand, whilst everyone from Yorkshire is a miserable bastard. The only saving graces of the entire north are the chips and the meat and potato pies. The rest, as far as I am concerned, is all crap.

Of course, I have no doubt that almost anyone from the north feels exactly the same as I do when they head south and, to a certain extent, such prejudices and bigotry are part and parcel of being a geezer. In fact, for me they are some of the more attractive features.

Yet whilst going north is a problem I must live with, the fact remains that there are pitfalls to our chosen lifestyle. Such pitfalls are an integral feature of the lifestyle of any geezer and you, as a relative newcomer, will soon come to know, understand and then accept all of this. But, to be perfectly honest, the pros far outweigh the cons. Having spent a lifetime hating L*t*n, the north and John Aldridge, I may not be able to wear orange, watch *Coronation Street* or laugh at Jimmy Tarbuck, but I sure as shit wouldn't miss the rest of it for anything. And, having come this far, neither would you.

Chapter Nineteen

The Future

So you've made it. If you've got this far and absorbed everything I've told you, you're ready to enter, if not already inside, the world of the geezer. And it is a wonderful place. A magical land filled with lads, lager and footie.

For the geezers, the future is rosy. Very rosy. After all, we survived the '70s and '80s with ease and are positively thriving in the caring, sharing '90s. The clothes are better, the money more plentiful and the travel far easier. It can only get better. All this despite the best efforts of both football and the Old Bill, who continue to hate us with a passion. Their continuing desire to remove us from football is doomed to failure because they simply do not realise that staying one step ahead of authority is, and always has been, a part of the great game we call geezerdom.

Yet while the geezers positively flourish, the same cannot be said of our great game. Make no mistake, there are problems on the horizon.

To the outsider, it would seem that football has changed out of all recognition in recent years. The hooligans have gone, as have the fences and the terraces, to be replaced by all-seater stadia, satellite television and corporate entertainment. The great game is better now than it has ever been. It has apparently undergone a revolution.

But it hasn't. It's exactly the same. It's still 22 men punting a plastic ball from one end of a pitch to the other. That, at least, will never change. What has changed out of all recognition is the way the game is marketed. These days, it's all face painting and families, sponsorship and stock markets. Some would argue that all of this is a good thing. That what we are witnessing is a post-hooligan evolution of the great game. But this, to use a well-worn phrase, is bollocks. The people who put forward such arguments are usually those who don't go, those who enjoy hospitality packages or those who work in the media. As most football fans with any degree of common sense will readily acknowledge, what we are actually witnessing is an explosion of greed.

Those running the game that we, as both supporters and geezers, actually continue to fund have realised that they have been given a golden opportunity. An opportunity which will, like all such golden opportunities, eventually disappear up its own arse and then vanish altogether. As a consequence of this, they are bleeding everything they can from it – and therefore us – until that time comes. And after that, they'll be gone. On to the next sport or, to be more accurate, the next business opportunity. Then, when the bubble has burst and the city money has been pulled out, football will be left with its head spinning, wondering what the bloody hell happened.

But in the meantime, while football is still the most marketable commodity on the planet, the money and marketing men continue to search for ever more inventive ways to get money out of the average working bloke. And we fall for it. Every single time. Replica shirts are the classic example of this but an even better illustration of greed triumphing over common sense can be demonstrated by the unrelenting drive towards the European Super League.

Up to now, for most of the clubs who make it, European competition has always been seen as a bit of a diversion. A reward for success in league or cup, of course, and a chance for the fans to travel abroad with their clubs once in a while and celebrate those achievements. But, ultimately, with a few obvious exceptions, European football is a change from the more important day-to-day business of the domestic battle. But not any more. Now the money men want to bring all the biggest, most successful teams in Europe together and pit them against each other in the ultimate league. Not just once in a while, but all of the time. This, they argue, will ultimately be good for the British game and therefore good for the national sides. Our football will, in the long term, benefit. Bollocks it will.

Forget all that. This isn't about football at all, it's about television. Because that's where the money is. And we're talking millions here. Millions and millions. All money to go on to the gravy train they call football. And, rest assured, that money will be swallowed up by the City or find its way into the pockets of various agents, directors and players. It certainly won't go into subsidising travel or cheaper ticket prices for the long-suffering fans, that's for sure.

Of course, we weren't asked about this. Because, as fans, our opinions don't count. All this stuff about it being good for the future of the national game is bullshit. How can Manchester United and Arsenal leaving the Premiership be a good thing? And what will happen to the rest when Celtic or Rangers desert the Scottish game? It'll be good for those who get in, of course, but it will certainly screw the rest. Even the fans of the clubs who make it will be shafted. How many midweek trips to Barcelona or Rome will the average United fan manage during a season, do you think? And as much as the Spurs fans hate Arsenal, I guarantee that they'd still rather see their lads play them twice during a season than only on the telly.

Outside the Premiership, or do I mean the European Super League Division One (England), it'll be even worse. The current first division may get away with it, but the rest? No chance. Welcome to Division Two South – part-time, of course.

For the armchairs this will be heaven-sent, because what we are really talking about is the ultimate armchair league. Arsenal versus Real Madrid, Manchester United versus Juventus, week in, week out. It's the stuff of wet dreams. And when there's no European game on, well, they might as well tune in to the small matter of Chelsea versus Liverpool in what used to be the greatest league in the world. The only problem they'll have is finding the time to watch all the games on offer and coming up with the huge amounts of money that they'll need to pay for the subscription.

Television is also behind the other big black cloud on the horizon: pay-per-view. This idea is so fucking ludicrous it beggars belief. Call me a cynic, but as a Watford fan the very last thing in this entire world I would ever want to do is pay an extra few quid to my local cable operator so that he can send highlights of Coventry versus Wimbledon down my fibre optics. That is assuming I have ever been stupid enough to fork out a small fortune to purchase a television capable of receiving digital television. I know there are some who would, of course, but, let's be honest here, who in their right mind – other than a Leeds United fan, of course – would want to watch Leeds United TV? No fucker, that's who. And yet they're all sprinting towards it as quickly as they possibly can. As if it's the pot at the end of the rainbow. I mean, other than the actual games, what are they going to show on it anyway? If most club-call lines are anything to go by, the average football club has trouble finding anyone able to speak coherently, never mind appear on telly. Let's face it, there are probably only two or three clubs in Britain who could pull off pay-per-view, and I would think that only Manchester United and possibly Rangers would ever make any money out of it. After all, given the armchair following of both these clubs, either of them could give *Eastenders* a run for its money in the ratings.

Yet the biggest problem of all currently facing football is that as it embraces television ever tighter, the time is rapidly approaching when supporters begin to realise that it just isn't worth going to games any more. It is cheaper, and easier, to simply go down the pub and watch the game while having a few beers. In most cases it will be with the same group of geezers and so the atmosphere will be as good, if not better, than at the actual game. For those who run football, this should be a major concern. Not only will it mean lost revenue in the short term, but, let's be honest, going to football is habit-forming and addictive. If you break that habit, especially if you discover another one, it is unlikely that you will ever go back. You will be lost to the game for ever. As a consequence, the income at the gate drops, which also means less money from catering and merchandise. This in turn leads to less sponsorship, and so on. But more of a worry is the fact that if the geezers stop going, the atmosphere dies. And when that happens, it's all over. Football really will be like going to the pictures or the theatre. No more singing, no more abusing, just a polite round of applause every time a goal is scored.

Some would argue that this will never happen. That football will always be the working man's ballet and that our love affair with the live game will never end. But they are wrong. The shift towards a culture of pub supporting has already started and the England side has suffered more than most. The crowds at many of the recent Wembley games have been embarrassing, what support there is being made up almost entirely of school kids and families with the result that the atmosphere, and noise, has been like a Spice Girls concert. Walk two miles down the road, though, and the pubs are rammed out, with geezers. All watching the game on Sky. Similarly, at a number of Premiership clubs, where season tickets are like gold dust and even tickets for away games are allocated by ballot, geezers are simply not going any more. They still meet up, though, and simply go to the nearest pub. Better to be in the company of your mates and watch the game on television than to spend an afternoon in the company of anoraks and new-breeds.

Of course, talk of pay-per-view and European Super Leagues means nothing if you support York City or Cambridge United. For outside the world of the fabulous wages and huge operating losses that is the Premier League, nothing has changed at all. At most clubs there are no shareholders to worry about and no share price to keep an eye on. Just directors and chairmen. The majority of whom, despite what you may think, have the best interests of the club at heart. Oh yes, they try and shaft their supporters just as much as the boys at the top, but if they step too far out of line, the supporters will let them know. Even the grounds have remained the same: crap toilets, awful food and, if you go low enough down the Football League, you can even find terraces. Because it is down outside the Premiership that the true spirit of British football lies. Down here, you go to football not to see quality but because you have a love of your club and the great game. That, at the end of the day, is what it's really all about. But, just as importantly, it is down in the basements of football that the true value of the geezer is recognised. Down here, the clubs know that when we geezers go to football we pay the full whack at the gate and then, once we are inside the ground, create a type of atmosphere that is unique to the British game. They appreciate the fact that we support them and respect the fact that we travel. In short, our presence is acknowledged and valued by the club that we choose to follow. If the lower leagues can teach the Premiership anything, it is this.

Yet, at the end of the day, none of this really matters. None of it at all. As geezers, we value ourselves and our mates above everything and know that our support is not just for the team, it's for the club. And that support is total and lifelong; screw everything and everyone else. How many of the new-breed army will still be walking through those turnstiles at Blackburn Rovers or even my beloved Watford if, God forbid, they suffer the ignominy of successive relegations? Ask Manchester City fans what supporting a football club really means, and while you're there look around and see how many of them are geezers. Almost all of them. That's how many. You see, anyone can walk through a turnstile with their faces painted and wave a scarf around to support their team. What we do is more than that. We not only support, we enhance. When a geezer walks down the road, he may spread envy, fear or loathing, but when he passes through those turnstiles, he brings class, passion, noise and humour. All things that come from a lifetime of patronage. Football is better because of, not in spite of, the presence of the geezers. And it bloody well knows it.

Long live the great game that is football and long live the geezer.

Part Seven

The Performance

Annex A

The Songs

Singing is, as we have seen, one of the most enjoyable aspects of being a football fan. For the geezers, these songs are invariably abusive and are almost always directed at opposing fans or players. This is a good thing. After all, football provides one of the few arenas available to the average male where being abusive is totally acceptable. Therefore, as long as that abuse is good-humoured, not to mention creative, it should be encouraged.

I have taken the liberty of supplying you below with the lyrics of a number of songs, as well as details of where, when and how they are sung. I must, however, warn you that some of these songs will not be sung at every club. Indeed, breaking out into a chorus of 'I'm Forever Blowing Bubbles' on the Kop at Anfield may not go down too well. This is not, however, a definitive list. Football fans are an imaginative breed and will adapt any song to suit their purposes. Be it to support their own team or to abuse someone else's.

As you will notice, many of the songs surround my own club, Watford, and our traditional dislike of our local rivals, Scum Town. This is because, as a Watford fan, I am familiar with these tunes and do not really care what any other club sings. However, to avoid any confusion and/or violence, please remember to substitute your own particular team.

LITTLE BOY
This is a simple chant mainly used to keep everyone singing when things get a little boring. The tune is loosely based around

that old Chuck Berry classic 'My Ding-a-ling':

When I was a little boy
My Daddy brought me a brand new toy
A L*t*n fan on a piece of string
He told me to kick his fuckin' 'ead in

Fuckin' 'ead in
Fuckin' 'ead in
He told me to kick his fuckin' 'ead in

Fuckin' 'ead in
Fuckin' 'ead in
He told me to kick his fuckin' 'ead in

A similar song is frequently heard at Watford but the tune is different. It's that old favourite 'Que Será, Será':

When I was just a little boy
I asked my Mummy, what should I be?
Should I be Watford, or L*t*n T*wn?
Here's what she said to me
Wash your mouth out son
And go get your father's gun
And shoot some L*t*n scum
Shoot some L*t*n scum

We hate L*t*n
We hate L*t*n

OH HERTFORDSHIRE!
Another simple chant. Usually used when you're on an away trip to let the 'home' fans know that you're better than they are. Sung to 'When the Saints Go Marching in':

Oh Hertfordshire, is wonderful!
Oh Hertfordshire, is wonderful!
It's full of tits, fanny and the Hornets
Oh Hertfordshire is wonderful

Conversely, the following version is equally popular:

Oh Bedfordshire, is full of shit
Oh Bedfordshire is full of shit
It's full of shit, shit and more shit
Oh Bedfordshire is full of shit

Indeed, excrement, Bedfordshire and L*t*n T*wn seem to figure in a number of Watford songs for some reason, although, again, any of the following can be adapted to your own club:

You're the shit, you're the shit,
You're the shit of Bedfordshire
You're the shit of Bedfordshire

Very loosely based around 'Bread of Heaven' or alternatively and to the same tune:

You're the shit, you're the shit,
You're the shit of everywhere
You're the shit of everywhere

Another song of a similar nature, sung to the tune 'Go West' by The Pet Shop Boys, is:

You're shit, and you know you are
You're shit, and you know you are (repeat endlessly)

MY OLD MAN . . .
Another simple anti-L*t*n chant, sung to the tune of 'My Old Man':

My old man
*Said be a L*t*n fan*
I said fuck off, bollocks
You're a cunt!

EVERYWHERE WE GO
One of my all-time favourite footie songs – well, more of a

chant, really. Sadly, it is rarely heard these days:

Everywhere we go
People wanna know
Who the hell we are
So we gotta tell 'em
We are the Watford
We play in black and gold
And if you wanna argue
Come and have a go

The Watford
The Watford

WE HATE . . .

Another traditional chant aimed at local rivals is the following ditty sung to an unknown tune:

We hate L*t*n and we hate L*t*n,
We hate L*t*n and we hate L*t*n,
We hate L*t*n and we hate L*t*n,
We are the L*t*n haters
We hate L*t*n
We hate L*t*n

GRAHAM TAYLOR . . .

This is one of those chants that has numerous variations and will break out at odd times during the game. I have listed below three of the versions we use at Vicarage Road to give you the general idea:

Graham Taylor's yellow army (repeat endlessly)

Graham Taylor's having a party
Bring your vodka and Bacardi (repeat endlessly)

Elton John's Taylor-made army (repeat endlessly)

LIVERPOOL SLUMS

An old and established favourite amongst football fans

everywhere. Sung to the tune of 'My Liverpool Home', it can be adapted to be abusive towards anyone and should be accompanied by mass pointing at the opposing fans while you sing it:

In your Liverpool slums
In your Liverpool slums
You look in a dustbin for something to eat
You find a dead cat and you think it's a treat
In your Liverpool slums

BUBBLES
The theme tune of West Ham United. This song should never be sung in this form by anyone else. Ever.

I'm forever blowing bubbles
Pretty bubbles in the air
They fly so high
Nearly reach the sky
Then like my dreams
They fade and die
Fortunes always hiding
I've looked everywhere
But I'm forever blowing bubbles
Pretty bubbles in the air

United . . . United

There is one variation of this song which is adaptable to any club and their local rivals. It is written below:

I'm forever blowing bubbles
Pretty bubbles in the air
They fly so high
They reach the sky
And like Tottenham
They fade and die
Arsenal's always running
L*t*n's running too
And Watford's always running,

Running after you

The Watford
Watford

NO ONE LIKES US

Sung to the tune of the Rod Stewart hit 'Sailing', this song has become the theme tune of Millwall supporters everywhere. If you follow any other club and value your health, you should never even think about singing it. Even when you're on your own and miles from any civilisation:

We are Millwall, we are Millwall
We are Millwall, from The Den
We are Millwall, super Millwall
We are Millwall, from The Den
No one likes us, no one likes us
No one likes us, we don't care
We are Millwall, super Millwall
We are Millwall, from The Den

GLORY, GLORY

Sung to the tune of 'Glory, Glory Hallelujah', this song used to be a favourite at Vicarage Road. However, it now seems to have settled into life at Tottenham, although it has been heard at almost every club in the land at some time or another. This is the Watford version:

Glory, glory Watford FC
Glory, glory Watford FC
Glory, glory Watford FC
And the 'Orns go marching
On, on, on!

HE'S ONLY A POOR . . .

A great song for firing up the geezers. Written below are two variations of this song, although it has been heard in many forms over the seasons. The first is the traditional Watford version, the second is from West Ham. It is sung to a tune called 'The Sparrow':

He's only a poor little Hatter
His face is all tattered and torn
He made me feel sick
So I hit him with a brick
And now he won't sing any more (repeat only once)

or:

He's only a poor little Cockney
His colours are claret and blue
And one day this season
For no fucking reason
He's gonna kick fuck out of you

IF I HAD THE ARSE . . .
A firm favourite at local derby games. Sung to the tune of 'My Bonny Lies over the Ocean', this is guaranteed to fire up the home fans every time:

If I had the wings of a sparrow,
If I had the arse of a crow
I'd fly over L*t*n tomorrow
And shit on the bastards below, below
I'd shit on the bastards below
Shit on, shit on
I'd shit on the bastards below, below
Shit on, shit on, I'd shit on the bastards below

BLUE MOON
One of the great football songs, 'Blue Moon' is merely a rendition of a musical classic that has become synonymous with Manchester City (or, for that matter, almost anyone who plays in blue). When the City fans are in full cry, this song never fails to bring a tear to the eye of true football fans everywhere:

Blue moon, you saw me standing alone
Without a dream in my heart
Without a love of my own

Blue moon, you knew just what I was there for
You heard me saying a prayer for
Someone I really could care for

Then suddenly they'll appear before me
The only one my arms could ever hold
I heard someone whisper 'please adore me'
And when I looked, my moon had turned to gold

Blue moon, now I'm no longer alone
Without a dream in my heart
Without a love of my own

Tragically, this song has been bastardised more than once as opposing fans use it to have a pop at City. Usually I would applaud that, but this song is so great I will not talk of these versions ever again.

WHO ATE ALL THE PIES?
Sung to the tune of 'Knees Up, Mother Brown', this song has become a firm favourite with fans everywhere. Primarily used to have a go at people who are calorifically challenged (or, in other words, fat), it is accompanied by pointing at the individual being targeted:

Who ate all the pies?
Who ate all the pies?
You fat bastard, you fat bastard
You ate all the pies!

WE'RE ON THE MARCH
Another firm favourite, this song, to the tune of 'Ally's Tartan Army', appears almost everywhere in some form or another.

Here is just one variation from Vicarage Road:

We're on the march with Taylor's army
We're not going to Wemb-er-ly
And we don't give a fuck
'Cause the 'Orns are going up
'Cause Watford are the greatest football team

(repeat once, even louder)

WE'RE GOING UP . . .

Tragically, but sadly inevitably, that theme song of the armchair football fan 'Three Lions' has spawned numerous chants on the terraces of British football. Even worse, one of them is frequently heard at Watford, and here it is:

We're going up
We're going up
We're going
Watford's going up (repeat over and over)

GET YOUR TITS OUT!

Football grounds being the havens for sexism that they thankfully are, the odd song about the female of the species occasionally surfaces. 'Get your Tits out' is probably the best-known example of this. Best sung, and certainly most effective, as a female walks across the front of the stand, it can also be hugely amusing when sung at pubescent cheerleaders during half-time. However, this practice should not be encouraged, as it is pretty sick. Sung to the tune of 'Bread of Heaven', the lyrics are simple ones:

Get your tits out
Get your tits out
Get your tits out for the lads
Get your tits out for the lads

JINGLE BELLS

Football songs can also provide the kiss of death to a club, as a few of them are inevitably jinxed. A good example of this is 'Jingle Bells'. Any rendition of this song inevitably means that, within seconds, the opposing club will score. Therefore it should never be sung until after the final whistle has gone:

Jingle bells, Jingle bells
Jingle all the way
Oh what fun it is to see
Watford win away
Oh! (repeat)

MY MOTHER'S . . .

One of the great things about football fans is that they will often adopt songs that have little or nothing to do with football. Below are two such examples, and although they are best-known at Hartlepool and Chelsea, variants have been heard at numerous clubs up and down the leagues:

My brother's in Borstal
My sister's got pox
My mother's a whore down in Hartlepool Docks
My uncle's a pervert
My aunty's gone mad
And the Yorkshire ripper's my dad

(sung to the tune of 'Just One of Those Songs')

Celery, celery
If she don't come
I'll tickle her bum
With a stick of celery

(tune unknown)

Finally, single-line chants are always good value as they are usually targeted at visiting supporters. What follows are just a few of the ones you will inevitably hear during your time as a geezer. For example, if you are away and the home fans are quiet:

You're supposed to be at home,
You're supposed to be at home

Or, if the visiting fans are few and far between:

Come in a taxi
You must have come in a taxi
Come in a taxi
You must have come in a taxi

If an opposing player does something clearly not very good, this should be sung to the tune of 'Knees Up, Mother Brown':

You're not very good
You're not very good
You're not very
You're not very
You're not very good

There are a huge number of these chants used at football these days. For example, if the visiting club have either a crap ground or crap support:

What's it like to see a ground? (or *a crowd*)

Or, if the opposition are shit:

What's it like to be outclassed?

If your lads are losing, you may well hear the opposing supporters singing the following song in an effort to wind you up:

Sing when you're winning
You only sing when you're winning
Sing when you're winning
You only sing when you're winning

If you hear this song, the simple response should be:

We're always winning

Another chant to throw at the opposing fans when they start to get a bit vocal is:

Who are ya?
Who are ya?

A variation of which is:

Who the fucking hell are you?
Who the fucking hell are you?

Lastly, the chants most frequently heard at Watford in recent months are the following:

One-nil, to the golden boys (repeat over and over)

Stand up, if you're top of the league (repeat)

and

Stand up, if you're going up (repeat)

Annex B

The Gestures

Gesturing, alongside singing, chanting and abusing, is another valuable weapon for the geezers. Not only is it highly visible, it is also hugely entertaining and has the added bonus of ensuring that your blood is circulating and you can keep warm. On a cold, wet terrace in the middle of December, this is not just important, it is vital.

Gestures fall into two main categories. The first of these is basic hand and arm movements for use inside grounds, whilst the second is posturing. These are for use mainly outside grounds and the majority are primarily used to show either your arrogance or your bottle.

What follows are descriptions of the main gestures, what they mean and, if appropriate, when to use them. It should not, however, be thought of as definitive. As you will quickly realise, football fans not only lose all sense of rational thinking when inside a football stadium, some of them also lose all control of their bodies.

Like everything else discussed in this book, it is best to practise these gestures at home before going to an actual game. Again, if you have a video camera, film yourself doing these actions and compare them to the actions of your peers during one of your research visits to your chosen ground. The old maxim 'practice makes perfect' certainly applies here.

HAND AND ARM GESTURES

These, as the title implies, are gestures carried out using just the hands and the arms. For this reason they are perfect if you have to sit down, although, as you should be aware by now, no geezer worth his salt sits down at football.

THE WANKER SIGN

One of the geezers' favourites, this gesture is designed to intimate that the target recipient is either fond of masturbating or is simply not very good. The beauty of this signal is that it can be used to abuse players, other fans or even the officials and is so universal it need not even be accompanied by any words. It is, however, usually done in conjunction with a strange 'arrrgh' noise and a glare at the offending individual. It is particularly effective when an opposing player has made a mistake of some kind, although it can be used at any time.

To make this gesture, fully outstretch your arm (either left or right) in front of you and form your index finger and thumb into a circle. Holding your hand parallel to your body, move your hand swiftly up and down as if you were shuffling dice.

Alternatively, with your arm close in to your body, bend your elbow to about 60 degrees so that your hand is at cheek height, form your hand into a tight fist and then relax it to form a tunnel between your palm and your fingers. You should then move your hand with the same shuffling motion as above.

Making the motion whilst holding your hand in front of your groin is not a good idea. Not only is there the chance that the target may not see the gesture if your hand is low down, there is also the very great possibility that the other geezers nearby may think the movement is familiar to you.

THE V SIGN

Another great favourite amongst the geezers. In this context, however, it does not mean victory; it means 'Fuck off' and can be used at any time either inside or outside grounds.

To make this gesture, simply hold your hand in front of you at chest height and with the palm towards you (unlike Mr

Churchill's version) extend the fore and middle fingers to form the letter V whilst folding the thumb and remaining fingers into the palm.

Once this has been done, the hand should be moved up and down through about six inches. Alternatively, the arm can be kept still and some degree of motion achieved by pivoting the hand at the wrist, not just moving the fingers, as it is more visible. It is also particularly effective if you use both hands.

Again, there is no vocal accompaniment to this sign, although you can always merely mouth the words 'Fuck off', which seems to work quite well.

THE FINGER

In recent years, following the intrusion – sorry, I mean explosion – of American culture into Britain, 'the finger' has made strong inroads into the geezer's armoury. Personally I am unhappy about the appearance of this gesture, as we Anglo–Saxons have always been famous for our expletives and the importation of anyone else's fills me with disgust. Especially an American one.

However, if you must make this gesture, it is achieved by simply holding out the hand in front of you at face height with the palms towards you. You then extend the middle finger so that it points directly upwards. No other movement is required.

Again, a simple 'Fuck off' or even a 'Fuck off, you wanker' will suffice if you need to say something.

POINTING

Many of the songs you will hear, and eventually sing, at football are accompanied by pointing. This can be directed either at opposing players or at supporters, depending on who the chant is aimed at. It will not be too difficult to work out which songs these are, as the moment the singing starts, everyone else will begin to point. However, as a rule of thumb, any song which contains the word 'you're' or 'you' will require this gesture, for example 'You're shit, and you know you are' or 'Sing when you're winning, you only sing when you're winning'.

Pointing is relatively easy, even for the novice. Just before the first word of the song (the command word), the arm should be raised to chest height and then bent at the elbow to pull the hand back towards the shoulder. Then, on the command word, form the hand into a fist and, with the forefinger extended, flick the hand forwards, extending the arm and pointing at the target. The hand should then be left until the start of the next line in the chant, when the motion should be repeated. This should continue until the chant has finished. It is vital to remember that you only do this with one hand at a time or you will look ridiculous.

THE WHIP

This gesture is used primarily to accompany songs which include the words 'Come on', for example 'Come on you 'Orns' or 'Come on Watford'.

It is exactly the same as pointing but in this instance is aimed in the general direction of the pitch.

ARMS WIDE

Another gesture you will frequently observe amongst the geezers is standing up with both arms outstretched to the side. This is done when the opposing forwards fail to hit the goal with either a header or a shot and it is used to signal your derision at their inaccuracy. It is usually accompanied with the traditional 'arrrgh' shout or even a loud 'whooooooo', although recently this gesture has been made whilst singing the following:

How wide (or high) *do you want the goal?* (repeat)

A variation of this is to hold your arms out directly in front of you and then swing them round so that they are stretched out to the side. This should be repeated a few times while singing the above song.

ANGER

Sadly, it is inevitable that during a game one of the players or officials will do something that will make you angry. For example, one of your own players will miss an open goal, an opposing player will foul one of your team or the referee will make a decision that you do not necessarily agree with. When this happens, you will see a number of the geezers frantically waving their arms about whilst screaming abuse at the offending individual.

There is no established format for this. It is very much an individual thing. For example, some geezers will throw both hands up into the air and then point angrily; others will hold their hands above their head and then throw them forward in exasperation. A select few will merely clutch their head in their hands whilst turning round and round.

All I can advise is that you watch the other geezers for a while and then adopt a gesture of your own. Whatever it is, as long as you do it when everyone else is also furious, no one will notice.

THE PUNCH

This is a dual-purpose gesture. It can be used either to signify your anger at something or to urge someone on (i.e. a winger hurtling down the line) and is particularly effective when being done by a large number of geezers at the same time.

To do this, raise your right arm as if you were saluting someone and then, with your hand in a tight fist, move it in a circular motion as quickly as you can just forward of your shoulder. Whilst you do this, if you are registering your unhappiness at someone or something, you should lean slightly forward and hurl torrents of incoherent abuse at the offending individual. If, however, you are urging a player on, you should shout 'Go on' but form the two words into a single one by substituting the second letter 'o' for an 'r'. This will make the word 'Gorn', which should be shouted repeatedly and at full volume. You should only ever make this gesture with one hand at a time.

WAVING (OR CHEERIO)

Another gesture designed to wind up opposing fans, waving has two main purposes. The first is when opposing fans are leaving early and is accompanied by the chant:

We can see you sneaking out (sung to 'Bread of Heaven')

The second is when your club is about to be promoted and the opposition is not or, similarly, the opposing club is about to be relegated. Some supporters will use this when they are about to be relegated, but as a geezer you will be far too gutted to indulge in such irony.

A third use for waving is when an opposing player has been sent off. However, this can only really be used if you are anywhere near the tunnel area as the player walks off and, in any case, as a geezer the wanker sign is far more suitable here.

To wave, simply extend your arm so that it is stretched out in front of you, stare at the target and move your hand from side to side vigorously.

NAIL BITING

From time to time, when a game is exciting, you may well see various people, even the odd geezer, biting their nails. There is nothing wrong with this at all. After all, geezers are football fans and football is a passionate and often tense business. If someone near to you is biting his nails, only ever point it out if he starts drawing blood. If, however, you are ever at a game and someone starts biting your nails, I would leave at once.

SORROW

Thankfully a gesture rarely seen at Watford these days, but it can frequently be witnessed at L*t*n T*wn. Especially when the Watford result is read out. Also known as holding your head in your hands, this gesture is achieved by merely sitting down, dropping your head on to your knees and placing your hands either side of your head whilst staring at the floor. Alternatively, you can merely sit down, lean forward and rest your chin in the palms of your hands while staring ahead through either glazed or moist eyes. In either case, once adopted, this position should be endured until the final whistle.

This gesture should only be used when things are going wrong, for example when your team are losing a local derby or when it has suddenly dawned on you that when you set out on the road of football fandom you should have chosen Vicarage Road and not Kenilworth Road.

GROVELLING

If you suddenly find yourself confronted by a steward or a policeman who has taken exception to something you have done or said, all you can do is grovel in the hope that he will think he has made a mistake. The beauty here is that as you protest your innocence – which, of course, you always should even if you are as guilty as sin – all the other geezers will jump in to back you up. After all, everyone hates authority and all geezers look after their own. This, for you, is a very good thing as it will enhance your standing amongst your peers.

If you are forced to grovel, always stand up. The reason for this is that if you remain seated, the official will be looking down on you, which is never a good thing. Then, with your arms out in front of you and your open palms facing upwards, protest your innocence by repeating the phrase 'What?' or 'What the fuck are you on about?'. Never, ever say you are sorry. No geezer should be sorry for anything.

An alternative to this is simply to tell the official to 'Fuck off' and, depending on the look on your face, which should be one that says 'Do you want to make anything of it?', he will probably leave you alone. However, this is not a good idea if the person standing in front of you is a policeman, for obvious reasons.

If, after your protests, the official does decide to leave you alone, it is imperative that the moment he turns his back on you you give him the wanker sign.

If an official does confront you, there is, of course, always the option of getting yourself thrown out (see 'Inside the Ground'). This should be considered if you're losing, the game is very boring or you support Spurs (which is much the same thing).

SORRY, MATE

A variation of 'grovelling', this gesture is used if you really did do something and were clearly caught red-handed. If this happens, simply hold your hands out in front of your body as if you were pushing something away from you and say 'Sorry, mate'.

'Sorry, mate' can also be used if you walk round a corner and bump slap, bang into the main hooligan firm of the opposing club. However, if this happens, the movement and dialogue are slightly different. After adopting the position, walk backwards whilst apologising profusely. If they approach you menacingly, you should then lie through your teeth about who and what you are. For example, simply point out that you do not want any trouble but are merely making your way home because you hate football. Alternatively, tell them that you have seen the other group and they are waiting for them in the next street. Do not tell them you are a 'Top Boy' from another firm recruiting for the biggest England crew ever seen and you have heard that they are really up for it. Or that you are an undercover policeman and they had better watch their step. Either of these will earn you a good kicking.

BOWING

The wannabes' favourite gesture, bowing is used to show a player that he is of god-like status. Therefore it should not be used by geezers, who all know that whatever a player does, it is never good enough for them.

To bow in the traditional football manner, simply hold your arms out to your side and then bend them through 90 degrees at the elbows as if you were surrendering. Then simply move your hands forward in a sweeping motion whilst bowing your head and leaning slightly forward. Then move them back to the original position and repeat until everyone else stops.

Finally, the ultimate example of this type of hand and arm gesture is the Mexican Wave. Thankfully, this has never caught on inside British football stadia and any future efforts to start it must be resisted. This can only be done by the geezers, who seem to be the only group of supporters who know how pathetic it looks. If it ever starts inside a ground where you are watching the game, be it your club or the national side, this is how to react.

When the wave reaches the area where you and the other geezers are sitting, merely stand up and look in the direction from whence it came and give them all either the wanker sign or a simple V sign. Then sit down. This will have the added bonus of upsetting all the anoraks and wannabes who love all that rubbish. They will begin to whistle and boo and then, after a short while, will try to start it again. The geezers should simply repeat their previous action and, eventually, the other supporters will give up.

POSTURING

Posture is as vital to geezers as their clothes. It shows that they are confident and cocky to the point of arrogance, which is, after all, one of the key elements of geezerdom. This posture is not just about the way you stand, but also about the way you walk and some of the things you will do, because to the outsider some of them make no sense at all. Indeed, it is also fair to say that the way you do something outside a ground will be different from the way you do it inside. The reason for this is simply that once inside a ground, any nagging doubt about that other group of geezers standing across the road will be removed.

It is also important to note that a number of the mannerisms you will see at football grounds, particularly outside, are influenced by the hooligans (see 'Hooligans'). Although I would urge anyone to avoid this type of behaviour at football grounds, if you intend to travel away with your club it is inevitable that at some point you will come across it. As we have seen, hooligans are simply geezers who take things a little too far. And so you need to know what they will do so that you can identify the problem when it arises and, more importantly, how you should react. It is important to remember, though, that outside grounds, especially at away games, you should always try to be within spitting distance of other geezers from your club.

Below are listed some of the more frequently used mannerisms and when and where they can be seen.

STANDING
Inside a ground, standing will be the position adopted to watch the game. Therefore all eyes will be on the pitch other than when hurling abuse at the opposing fans and so any movements will be dictated by what is happening on the field of play.

If you have to remain stationary outside a ground, however, the chances are it will be outside a pub or in a queue. In either case, always try and have something in your hands, be it a glass, a bottle or a cigarette, as this will keep them busy. If you have nothing to hold, always keep at least one hand in your pocket because, as any psychologist will tell you, having both hands visible and empty is a sign of vulnerability.

When you are standing still, always avoid slouching and keep your head up and your shoulders back, as this will project that much-needed air of confidence. You should also adopt an expression that reflects the fact that you are unhappy with being kept hanging about. It is also worth keeping an eye on what is going on around you, and it is best to do this by moving your head around fairly slowly as if you could not care less. This may well be difficult to achieve if you are playing Millwall at the New Den.

LOITERING

Although very similar to standing in style, loitering is in fact a favoured tactic of the geezer and, especially, the hooligan. It is particularly useful at train stations, outside grounds or near to pubs when the police are watching.

Its primary function is to let opposing geezers know that you are there, that you are ready and that you are waiting for them. This can either be for them to come and hurl abuse at you or for you to hurl abuse at them when they turn up. However, loitering is also useful for letting the police know where you are, which is vital if there are only a few geezers with you and you are in Stoke because the police will keep an eye on you and hopefully protect you.

Loitering is not as easy to do as it first appears, and the way it is actually done will be dependent on a number of factors. These range from being at home or away to the quality of the opposition. For example, if you are a Leicester City geezer and are at home to Wimbledon, there is no need to loiter at all and you should simply go into the pub. If, however, you are playing West Ham at home, loitering will consist of getting as many geezers as possible together, forming them into a tight group and staring up and down the road endlessly for any sign of approaching opposition. However, if you are away to Wimbledon, loitering will consist of grouping together outside local pubs and hurling abuse at locals, while if you're away at West Ham loitering will only take place as you wait to run off the buses into the ground.

Generally speaking, though, if you do want to indulge in a bit of loitering, it should be done before going to the ground and after going to the pub. That way you'll have a few beers inside you to boost your confidence.

The best way to loiter is to lean against something. Ideally this should be a pub, a wall or, in a perfect world, a police transit van. Legs should be slightly forward and crossed, while one hand should be occupied with a cigarette. If there are a good number of you, you should form a tight circle and keep looking around to spot the opposition supporters. When spotted, the group should stand up straight and either stare them out or, if there are only a few of them, begin hurling abuse until the police move you on. If you are with a group of hooligans you should run after them, because if they are hooligans they will run after you.

You should not try loitering on your own. It is strictly a group activity.

WALKING

The way you walk projects your self-assurance like a laser beam. It is also, aside from your clothes, the very first thing most people will ever notice about you and so you need to do it right. However, walking at football is not as simple as it sounds. After all, you're not going shopping here, you're going to football, and so you're showing out. Your walk is vital.

Inside a ground, the opportunities to walk around are obviously limited and so the adoption of the 'Liam Gallagher' walk is recommended (see 'Getting to your Seat'). However, outside is a whole different ball game. I mean, who would want to walk along their local high street looking that stupid on purpose?

To achieve the ultimate geezer walk, it is vital that you understand a few rules. The first is that you must keep moving. To a geezer, time is precious and waiting is wasted time. Always be doing something even if it's scratching your arse. Secondly, it is vital you avoid slouching or limping, as they are signs of weakness and/or illness. Even laughing should be avoided. Being a geezer is a serious business. The look on your face should reflect that.

Pull those shoulders back, lift your head up and take long and confident strides. A cigarette is essential and this should be held between thumb and forefinger, not between the fore and middle fingers. Too girlie. Your other hand should always be in your pocket. Talking is fine, as long as it's to other geezers, but even this should be done in moderation. If you have to stop, for example when the police are stopping traffic and/or fans, use that time to light another fag. If the one you have is barely started, dump it and light another.

When walking, never, ever stop for zebra crossings. These are for people who have problems crossing roads on their own. Or anoraks. If you come to a road, just walk straight out there and make your way through the traffic. If you glare at the drivers, they won't even sound their horns at you but will slow down and let you pass. If a car actually hits you, do not go down. Merely give the driver tons of abuse and kick at least one of his headlights in. Hopefully, the other geezers will do the rest. If this happens, he will not get out of his car.

As you near the ground, you should always cross from one side to the other and then back at least twice. There is no real reason for this but everyone does it.

THE SIDEWAYS GLANCE

At some time or another as you walk along, you will come across another group of geezers you do not recognise. This is when you use 'the sideways glance'. As you approach this group, do not slow down. Merely cross the road to be on the opposite side and, keeping your head to the front, move your eyes to the extreme side and glare at them. The reason for this is that they may be supporters of your own club whom you have not seen before and glaring at them full on may well cause a little friction.

If you do not recognise them, the best advice I can give is not to show even a flicker of emotion and to keep walking. If there are more of them than you, increase speed and head discreetly towards the nearest policeman. After a few years, or if you get in with some serious geezers, you will be able to simply walk straight through them. You should not, however, do this when you are on your own (see 'Hooligans').

LOOKING BEHIND

I would always advise you to keep a wary eye on your back as you walk along anywhere. This is especially important if you have just passed another group of geezers and used 'the sideways glance', as it is always best to keep an eye on what this other group do. The best way to do this is to be discreet. After all, caring about what others do can translate into being concerned and, as a geezer, you care not a toss about anyone else. However, the best way to look behind is through the dubious use of shop windows, or, if one is available, cast lustful eyes at young ladies who pass by you in the opposite direction. It never fails. If you do spot that you are being followed, again a discreet change of direction towards the nearest transit van full of Old Bill is always a good ploy.

COME ON, THEN!

This is similar in style to the 'arms wide' gesture used to signify a miss by an opposing player. However, in this context there is a subtle difference, as 'Come on, then' is used primarily to goad opposing fans and to invite them to come and have a go at you if they think they are hard enough.

Hold your arms out wide with the palms uppermost and the fingers outstretched. The fingers should then be folded into and out of the palms repeatedly. As you do this, you should bend your knees slightly so that you bob up and down, and you should also stretch your head forward a little. Occasionally, the shout 'Come on, then' can be used to accompany this movement.

This mannerism is best used outside grounds when there are far more of you than there are of them or when there is a large police presence between the two groups. It can also be used inside grounds and is particularly effective when standing on seats. If another group appears to be making this gesture towards you, if you are outside the ground you should merely give them the wanker sign. If you are inside, the usual response is to point at the individual making the gesture and then point in the vague direction of the streets outside. This is to signify that you will be seeing him when you get outside. Which, of course, you won't.

GIVING IT 'THE BIGGIE'

'The biggie' or 'the large one' is one of the classic geezer mannerisms and, like 'Come on, then!', is used to invite the opposing fans to cross the road to indulge in violence with you and your friends. As this gesture is so popular, it is vital that you know how to do it. Although rarely seen inside grounds these days, 'the biggie' can frequently be observed outside pubs on match days or even on train stations when the travelling fans arrive. It will also be in frequent use at any local derby and, like the 'Come on, then!', is best used when there is a large police presence and you know that the chances of the opposing fans actually getting near you are zero.

To effect this, hold your arms out in front of you as if you were holding a barrel. Then, lean back from the waist as far as you can, move the fingers rapidly, as if tickling a salmon, and thrust your head in and out at great speed while screaming 'Come on, then, you wankers'. The legs should be slightly bent and you can either take repeated steps backwards and forwards or bob up and down slightly. Alternatively, you can bounce around like a boxer on heat and then every so often run towards the opposing fans, or the police, before stopping and walking backwards to where you started. If there are a lot of you, a variation of this is to strut around between the two groups, but if you do this you should not look at the opposing fans but should stare at the ground as you shout. This is supposed to show that you are winding yourself up for an attack, when in actual fact you should be working out a way to get out of there and still save face.

'The biggie' can also look especially convincing inside grounds but only if you can move around freely. The reason for this is that, to be effective, all the geezers should be as close to the opposing fans as possible. This means moving from their seats down to the barriers separating the two groups. Once there, 'the biggie' should be adopted before the police and stewards arrive because, once there, they will drive everyone back to their original seats. If this happens, always join in. If you don't, questions may well be asked.

LUNGING
Another old favourite, lunging has largely been consigned to the history books as it is used to show aggression inside grounds and is very difficult to achieve now that most grounds are all-seater.

However, like all gestures, it occasionally surfaces, and in the case of lunging it will be if an opposing geezer or hooligan suddenly appears in your section of the ground. If this happens, all the geezers from your club will move rapidly in his direction. They will then lunge towards him with their fists outstretched in the vain hope that they will hit him and enhance their credibility amongst the other geezers. You should not do this.

Another opportunity for lunging will be if an opposition fan is taken out of the ground and walked across in front of where the geezers are sitting. As he traverses the section, the geezers will lunge towards him, hurling abuse or even throwing objects such as coins in his direction. You should not do this either.

RUNNING

As a geezer, running should be avoided at all costs. You should know where you're going, how long the journey takes and exactly how long you've got to get there. There are, however, exceptions to this rule, and these will almost certainly involve the influence of the hooligans.

We have already discussed the subject of hooliganism and, as a result, you will know when it is safe for you to run. Be it after or away. If that time arrives and you have to run after someone, run only as fast as you need to to maintain a safe distance between you and your 'victim'. If they slow, you slow. After all, you may be chasing them, but you certainly do not want to catch them. The exception to this is if the police turn up. At this time, safe in the knowledge that you will not actually have to hit anyone, you should accelerate into the arms of the waiting policemen, who will simply tell you to go away in some form or another.

If someone is running after you, you must forget all the rules of style and confidence and get away. Simply sprint as fast as you can to get as much distance between you and any actual violence as is possible. Do not stop until you are in actual physical contact with a policeman or your pursuer has stopped and has been left well out of sight. You should also forget any thoughts of guilt as a result of either your cowardice or your desertion. There isn't a situation known to man that is worth getting a black eye for. Not even geezerdom. The chances are that any other geezer who was with you as you walked into trouble will already have vanished into thin air by the time you decided to run. What do you think the proverb 'He who fights and runs away lives to fight another day' was invented for?

Glossary

This glossary, like many of the things contained in this book, has two functions. The first of these is to provide the novice geezer with a little help in understanding some of the more commonly used terms and phrases you will not only have read within this book but which you will also hear as you spend time with other geezers. The second function is to give you a little insight into the bigoted, sexist and élitist mind of both the average male football fan and, more importantly, your peers.

Therefore what follows is not just a little of the background information on such vital topics as non-league football and David Mellor, but thoughts and opinions on them. This should allow you to indulge in conversation with another geezer if the opportunity arises. However, a word of warning. The sentiments contained within this glossary are mine and they reflect my bigoted, élitist and above all sexist views. The geezer you meet up with the next time you travel to an away game may not be as enlightened as I am. Therefore his opinions on the subject of Zoë Ball may differ slightly from mine and he may well think she is fit. Even though anyone who thinks this is clearly troubled, it should not deter you from talking to him. After all, healthy debate is one of the joys of being in a pub with other footie fans. Just tread carefully rather than jumping in with all guns blazing and you'll be fine.

A

AFC Bournemouth: South-coast club best known for the fact that the great Luther Blissett once played there. Bournemouth are also the only club owned by the local community rather than by some money-grabbing chairman. For this alone, they deserve respect.

Aldridge (John): Scouse footballer. You know how you sometimes hate someone for no apparent reason . . .

Anderson (Clive): Overweight bald bloke off the telly and also celebrity football fan. 'Supports' Arsenal and is also a member of the legal profession. Therefore not to be trusted.

Anorak: A person who watches the game bedecked in replica shirts, scarves and stupid hats. Usually only children, old gits or Man United fans.

Armchair: Someone who talks endlessly at work about football but who actually supports 'their' team from the comfort of their front room whilst wearing their replica shirt. Usually Arsenal, Chelsea, Liverpool or Man United fans, as these are the more successful clubs and therefore are on telly the most. Best thought of as the scum of the earth. Pure and simple.

Arsenal: North London giants featured in your favourite book, film, play, board game and cuddly toy, *Fever Pitch*. Probably the most successful London club in recent years, Arsenal are to be respected and admired primarily because they keep Spurs fans, and therefore my old man, quiet. Play at Highbury.

Aston Villa: Midlands club run by mad dictator Deadly Doug Ellis. Most famous for being visible from the M6 motorway which just about sums them up. Play at Villa Park.

B

Baddiel (David): Professional 'celebrity' fan. One half of the so-called comedy duo Skinner and Baddiel (see Skinner and Baddiel). Apparently 'supports' Chelsea.

Baker (Danny): Professional cockney bloke and all-round top man. Original (and best) host of *606* but got the sack after advising supporters to have a go at referees. A true Millwall fan and therefore a proper geezer.

Ball (Zoë): Host of Radio One Breakfast Show and the ultimate geezer-bird. So desperate to be liked by everyone, she became a celebrity footie fan (of Man United, who else?) and then, to prove how much she knows about the game, brought out a book about the sexiest footballers in the Premier League. This merely reinforced the theory that she's a bit dim, really. A bit rough as well.

Barnsley: Yorkshire club who became everyone's second-favourite team when they made it to the Premier League, were spanked almost every week and were then relegated. Oh yes, and after their fans went ballistic against Liverpool and caused the referee to throw his teddy out of the cot and walk off the pitch. Still, if a club has a bulldog on their badge, what else can you expect? Play at Oakwell.

Bates (Ken): Owner and top man at Chelsea FC. Commonly referred to as the mad dictator by those from outside the club (and a few within it). However, given the quality of players, the fantastic ground and the amount of silverware the club has accrued in recent years, I get the distinct impression he does know what he's doing.

Beckham (David): Professional footballer with Manchester United. Young, brilliant, good-looking, loaded and with a pop star girlfriend. And people wonder why supporters hate him? Mind you, getting sent off against Argentina wasn't the best public relations stunt I've ever seen.

Birmingham City: Massive club currently fast asleep in the West Midlands. Supported by hordes of mad Brummies, the club is most famous for its hooligan firm 'The Zulu Army' and most infamous for the fact that it has a woman on the board! Play at St Andrews.

Blissett (The Great Luther): The greatest ever Watford player and my all-time footballing hero. Never gave less than 110 per cent and scored numerous priceless goals for the glorious Hornets. He even managed to put a tear in my eye when he scored a hat-trick for England at Wembley against Luxembourg. What more can you ask of your centre forward? Oh, for just one more season.

Bollocks: The favourite word of all true geezers everywhere. This is because it has numerous meanings and can be either aggressive or humorous, for example 'That's bollocks' (You're talking rubbish, officer) or 'It's the bollocks' (That's a very good pint, landlord). Strictly speaking, though, it means 'testicles'.

Bottle: Geezer's term for courage, as in 'He's got bottle' or 'That takes bottle'. The negative term for this is 'He's got no bottle' or 'He bottled it'. Someone who has no bottle is called a bottler, a tosser or a L*t*n T*wn fan.

Brentford: Club most famous for being on the flight path of Heathrow Airport and for having Chelsea do all their fighting for them (allegedly). Nothing else. Play at Griffin Park, which has a top chip shop round the corner opposite The Griffin pub.

Brighton and Hove Albion: Considering they've got two towns in their name it's somewhat ironic that they play in Gillingham because they've got no ground of their own. They've also got a kit that looks like a Tesco carrier bag. 'No hope, no future' should be the team's motto.

Bristol: The ultimate underachieving city, as it has two league teams, Rovers and City, both of whom have been crap in recent years. If you have a choice, the nearest decent team is Chelsea. They're only around two hours away by train and worth every second of the trip compared to these two no-hopers.

Brookside: Scouse soap. Not real.

C
Cardiff City: Welsh club known for their hatred of Swansea

City and everything English. Not the place to go and get mouthy.

Carlisle United: Club from the extreme north. The worst fixture in the world if you're doing every game in a season and Carlisle away is a Tuesday night in December. Or you support Plymouth.

Casuals: The original geezers. Ruled football during the late '70s and early '80s and were renowned for their expensive clothing. On the downside, the casual movement actually was football hooliganism. Great days, though, as anyone who was there will tell you.

Chamberlain (Helen): Blonde geezer-bird host of *Soccer AM* and therefore the anoraks' pin-up. Supports Torquay, which takes a bit of nerve, and actually does go, which also takes endurance. Looks a bit like Zoë Ball only slightly rougher.

Charlton Athletic: South London club most famous for losing its ground and then getting it back again. Supported by, amongst others, Jim Davidson, so laughs should be in short supply down at The Valley, which is where they play.

Chelsea: West London giants owned by mad dictator. The ultimate geezer club due to their location and history. The club is currently experiencing boom times as silverware arrives at the Bridge with sickening regularity. On the downside, they are also the favourite club of the oily git David Mellor and the oily twat David Baddiel. Play at Stamford Bridge.

Clarkson (Jeremy): Motoring journalist and television presenter from the BBC show *Top Gear*. Likes to think he is a geezer but is merely a mouthy public-school twat. Doesn't like football either, which also makes him a bit of a wanker as far as I'm concerned.

Corbett (Ronnie): Very short comedian well known for his love of golf and very lairy Pringle jumpers. The trend-setter for the original casual scene and well-known Crystal Palace fan.

Coventry City: Midlands club. Used to be run by arch television pundit and top bloke Jimmy Hill.

Crew: Slang term (similar to 'firm') for a group of hooligans allied to a particular club. Usually these groups will give themselves a nickname which will become synonymous with that club, for example 'The 657 Crew' (Portsmouth), 'The Blades Business Crew' (Sheffield United) and 'The Sly Crew' (Exeter City).

Crystal Palace: Crap club, crap area, crap kit and crap team. Play at Selhurst Park. Which is a crap ground.

D
Deayton (Angus): The bloke from *Have I Got News for You* and celebrity football fan of, surprise surprise, Man United.

E
Eastenders: Cockney soap. Not real.

Europe: Where Chelsea and Arsenal players learn their trade before coming over here and earning a fortune. Also the place where English and Scottish clubs go to be humiliated every single season. Except Chelsea, that is.

Evans (Chris): Ginger-headed media mogul. Owner of Virgin Radio (where he also works) and Ginger Productions and great mates with Danny Baker (whom he employs) and Gazza. Well-known supporter of all things footie and all-round top bloke.

Everton: The second club from Scouseland. Not as popular with the celebrities, nor with anyone else, for that matter. Certainly not with me after that bastard Andy Gray cheated us out of an FA Cup final win in 1984 when he bundled our keeper Steve Sherwood into the goal while he had the ball in his hands. And the ref only bloody gave it! Still, at least they hate Liverpool, which is something, I suppose. Play at Goodison Park.

Exeter City: Crap club supported by some top lads from the extreme West Country.

F

FA Cup: The world's oldest and greatest footballing competition.

Fanzine: Magazine put together by actual supporters in the comfort of their own bedrooms using their personal computers and with help from their Internet friends. Enough said.

Ferguson (Alex): Possibly the most successful British manager of all time. Sadly, he is currently at Manchester United and therefore disliked intensely by all football fans. Famous for his constant whinging about how everyone hates his club (which, of course, they do) and how every defeat United suffer is because they played badly or the referee was biased rather than because the other team were better.

Firm: Another slang term for a group of hooligans allied to a particular club. As with 'crews', these groups will give themselves a nickname which will become synonymous with that club, for example 'The Border City Firm' (Carlisle United), 'The Seaburn Casuals' (Sunderland) or 'The Naughty Forty' (Stoke City).

Football Task Force (The): Great idea. Go around the country talking to real football fans and getting their opinions on the game and what could be done to improve things. Sadly, the fact that it has David Mellor in charge and various new-breeds, do-gooders, academics and anoraks on the panel means it is doomed to failure. They could have achieved more if they had gone into my local pub.

Fowler (Robbie): Big-nosed Scouser who plays up front for Liverpool but supports Everton. Work that one out if you can.

France: Bastard nation from across the Channel who made a major-league cock-up of the ticket allocation for the 1998 World Cup, shafted all the England fans and then went and won the bloody thing! Oh yes, and they go on strike every chance they get, hold our lorry drivers to ransom, burn our lamb, ban our beef, eat snails and smell of garlic. Pity they weren't so stroppy in 1939.

Fulham: West London minnows doomed to a lifetime of living in the shadow of the great Chelsea. Literally, if Stamford Bridge gets any bigger. On paper, being owned by Harrods boss Mr Al-Fayed and run by Kevin Keegan should make them a big name, but the weak link is the fact that the team are crap. Play at Craven Cottage.

G

Gascoigne (Paul): Professional footballer and Geordie bloke known almost universally as 'Gazza'. Infamous for some of his less attractive off-field activities and currently plying his not inconsiderable talents at Middlesbrough. Former part-time genius (not to mention part-time liability) for England.

Geezer-bird: A woman who acts like a bloke. Because secretly she wishes she were one (see Ball or Chamberlain).

George (Boy): Music icon and now top DJ and journalist. Not a renowned football fan, although it is believed he is either an Iron or a Hatter.

Germany: Bastard country who always seem to beat us when it matters. That is except for 1918, 1945 and 1966 but, sadly, only one of those was at football.

Glasgow Celtic: Scottish club most famous for its hatred of Rangers and everything English.

Glasgow Rangers: Scottish club most famous for its hatred of Celtic and everything English.

Golden Days: The late '70s and early '80s. The time when geezers went to football on 'specials' and watched the game from terraces behind goals.

Grimsby Town: Most famous for singing 'Sing when we're fishing'. Nothing else, just that. Oh, and the town smells. Of fish.

Gullit (Ruud): Dutch dreadlocked footballing genius, star of Pizza Hut commercials and former Chelsea manager sacked by mad dictator which, as it turns out, wasn't a bad decision.

Gypo: An opposing player with long hair.

H

Halifax Town: Crap northern team now back in the Football League, which is a bastard if you support any other club in the third division because now you will have to go there.

Hancock (Nick): Stoke City's greatest celebrity football fan (which isn't saying much really) and star of crap TV quiz show *They Think It's All Over*, crap sitcom *Holding the Baby* and occasionally great TV show *Room 101*.

Hoddle (Glenn): Current England manager. Former great player for Spurs (yes, they used to have the odd one), then went on to manage Swindon Town and then Chelsea. Now widely known for putting his faith in God (the real one, not Le Tissier) and the odd healer rather than in his tactics and his players.

Hot Dog: The most beautiful-smelling item of food ever conceived. Often covered in onions and various sauces, most of which taste like vinegar (which is hardly a revelation considering that that will be what they were watered down with). Always overpriced and usually undercooked. Unless you are either drunk or have a liking for stadium toilets, avoid like the plague.

Hurst (Geoff): Former West Ham legend and scorer of the most famous hat-trick of all time (against West Germany in the 1966 World Cup final at Wembley).

Hurst (Lee): Bald bloke off *They Think It's All Over*. So-called comic but, actually, he's not very funny. No relation to the great Geoff Hurst.

I

Ince (Paul): England and Liverpool midfield general. Calls himself 'The Guv'nor', but more widely known as 'Judas'. Especially by West Ham fans after he left them to move to Man United.

Internationals: Fixtures between countries rather than clubs. Of the home nations, England are good, the rest are crap.

Italy: The land where everything decent ends in a vowel (i.e. pizza, Armani, Ferrari and footie) and the setting for the greatest ever World Cup tournament (Italia '90). It should, however, be noted that many fans of football (as opposed to football fans) think of Italian football as being the best in the world. This, as all geezers know, is bollocks. We invented the bloody game, and if their league is so good, why do they all come over here to play in ours?

J

James (David): Liverpool goalkeeper. Once played for Watford and nicknamed Dracula because he doesn't like crosses.

Jones (Vincent): Midfield general known as Vinny by all and sundry. Hated by the tabloids, he is loved by the geezers of every club he's ever played at as he never gives less than 100 per cent, which is all anyone ever wants. Incredibly, when he was starting out he was shown the door by Watford, who thought he was no good. He then went on to be the driving force behind Wimbledon's rise up through the Football League, resulting in an FA Cup triumph. Oh well, everyone makes mistakes.

K

Keegan (Kevin): Former Liverpool and England striker. Now manager of Fulham after long and successful spell at Newcastle. Most famous for permed hairstyle and shouting at Alex Ferguson.

Kop (The): Traditional home end at Anfield, where Liverpool play.

L

Lads (The): Blokes between the ages of 15 and 30 who, although almost as passionate and certainly as vocal as geezers, watch their football bedecked in Adidas, Ellesse and Umbro clothes rather than Duffer, Timberland or Stone Island. More importantly, they have yet to realise that they, as supporters, are more important to the club than the actual players. All geezers should realise that 'the lads' are the foot soldiers of football fandom and therefore they should be grudgingly respected and certainly acknowledged.

Le Tissier (Matt): Footballing genius and scorer of spectacular goals. Can do anything with a ball except have sex with it, and even that is probably open for debate. Plays for Southampton and should play for England. Always.

Leeds United: Yorkshire club renowned for teasing its own supporters (as in 'Will this be the season we actually win anything?') and its pathological hatred of Manchester United. Play at Elland Road.

Lesbian: See geezer-bird and women's football.

Leyton Orient: Underachieving club from south London. Most famous for being owned by snooker promoter Barry Hearn and loving the Queen Mum.

Lineker (Gary): Former goalscoring legend for England and regarded as Mr Nice Guy due to the fact he was never booked or sent off during his entire career. Now a television pundit and star of crap sports quiz *They Think It's All Over*. And some crisp adverts.

Liverpool: Scouse club currently clinging desperately on to a glorious past. Supported by hordes of professional scousers, including Cilla and Tarby, most of whom live in Surrey. Ironically near Cilla and Tarby. Play at Anfield, which actually is in Liverpool. Not Surrey.

Local Derby: The game all football fans hate because there is more than football at stake, there is also local pride. Ironically, not all local derbies involve clubs who are close together. For example, Watford's local derby is with Shit Town when, in actual fact, the club nearest to Vicarage Road is Barnet. Sadly, these games usually involve some degree of hooliganism, although, on the plus side, this can often be more entertaining than the actual match.

L*t*n T*wn: Also known as Shit Town or the scum. Scum ground, scum team and scum fans. Any links to this club are to be avoided at all costs. Nicknamed 'The Hatters' which, by a strange quirk of fate, is a slang term for homosexual (brown hatter).

M

McGrath (Rory): The hairy bloke off *They Think It's All Over* and also the only funny one. Apparently a lifelong and raving Arsenal fan, which is a bit odd because I was once told on very good authority that he used to hold a season ticket at Leeds United.

Manchester City: Laughing-stock team supported by some of the most loyal yet long-suffering football fans in the whole wide world. Let down by successive managers, chairmen and players. The club to support if you are an eternal optimist and live in Manchester. Play at Maine Road.

Manchester United: Probably the most successful British club in recent years and therefore hated and abused by everyone else. The club to support if you have a thick skin, like whinging, have a persecution complex, are an armchair or live in Ireland or Croydon. Not the club to support if you live in Manchester. Play at Old Trafford.

Match of the Day: Once-great football show now a shadow of its former self. Too much talking by too many ex-players equals not enough football.

Mellor (David): Ex-MP famous for sordid episode involving toes, dodgy women and Chelsea team shirts. Tragically, he is now the current host of BBC radio show *606* and is also head of the Football Task Force. This is because he is widely regarded as 'the fans' voice' by everyone except real football fans, who think he is a self-publicising arse. Once supported Fulham but now 'supports' Chelsea because Fulham are crap. Not to be taken seriously.

Middlesbrough: Yet another club from the north-east. Famous

Food Court
Food Court
Birmingham Airport

NCJE

Fruit salad   B   £2.99
Sunny delight   B   £1.43
Filter coffee   B   £1.20
Cappuccino   B   £2.95

Total   £7.03
CASH   £10.00
CHANGE   £2.97

GOODS @ 17.50% *   £5.98   £1.05

H.B. Caterers Group Plc.
28 Wilson Hospital, London BE1V B11
Vat No:GB 4EE 4777101

You were served by
Cashier 4
Term 1 Trn 22835 Cashier 1314
Unit 3 Date 10/08/2002 07:43

for achieving relegation from the Premiership and suffering Coca-Cola Cup final defeat in the same season. Oh yes, and then going back to Wembley the very next season and getting beaten again, ironically by the same team. Play at The Riverside, which is a stadium, not a pub.

Millwall: South-east London club renowned for its unruly supporters. Used to play at The Den, which was regarded as the roughest, toughest ground in the country, but moved to The New Den, which is now regarded as the roughest, toughest ground in the country. All Millwall fans are to be regarded as geezers. Even the women.

Mob: A group of geezers or hooligans on their travels (as in 'We were well mobbed up').

N

New-breed: Fans who have just discovered the great game and actually go. One step up from armchairs but still hated by the old school.

Newcastle United: Underachieving club from the far-flung north-east corner of England. Play in traditional kit of black and white stripes and have a huge and passionate support famous for creating massive amounts of noise. Sadly, in recent seasons the club has become more famous for the off-field antics of both managers and directors than the on-field success of the players. They have also suffered from an influx of new-breed supporters keeping out the locals. Play at St James' Park.

Non-League: Football for people who like to talk during games. Very boring and to be avoided at all costs if you have any kind of choice.

Norwich City: East Anglian club who play in yellow and green. To be hated if for no other reason than they have celebrity female football fan and cook Delia Smith as a director. Play at Carrow Road.

O

Off: Slang term as in 'It's going off', 'It went off' or 'There's been an off'. Means a confrontation between rival supporters who have a disagreement of some kind. Can also mean a sending-off (of a player), in which case it will be accompanied by the crowd shouting 'Off-off-off', or can even mean to be told to leave a location quickly (as in 'Fuck off').

Oldham Athletic: Northern club hated by me with a vengeance for some long-forgotten reason.

Osgood (Peter): Tall centre forward for Chelsea in the '70s and scorer of the most famous diving header of all time, the goal in the FA Cup replay against Leeds United in 1970. A god amongst men.

P

Peterborough United: Crap club from somewhere in the Midlands. Nicknamed 'The Posh', which is somewhat ironic as their ground resembles a collection of corrugated iron and scrap metal heaped together to form a large shed.

Pleat (David): Why?

Plymouth Argyle: Club from the south. Very dodgy ground and very dodgy fans. Still, if you live down there what choice have you got?

Police (The): Known universally as either the Old Bill or the Filth. The sworn enemy of geezers everywhere, as their role is primarily to spoil their enjoyment of the game. However, they are handy to have around when things look like turning nasty and there is even a remote possibility that you might get hurt.

Ponce: Also known as poncing. Means to scrounge off others without any intention of repayment, the worst practice known to man and totally alien to all true geezers.

Portsmouth: The biggest club in . . . Portsmouth. Known

throughout the game as Pompey and famous for the song 'Play up, Pompey, Pompey play up' (although I don't know why, as it's a crap song). Ironically, Pompey have indeed been known to play up a lot although, sadly, this isn't the team, it's the fans. Play at Fratton Park.

Premier League: The pinnacle of the English game. Loved by those clubs within it, hated by those outside it. This is where the money goes and this is where everyone wants to be.

Preston North End: Famous old club from somewhere up north. Best known in recent years for having a very nasty group of geezers amongst their support.

Programmes: Overpriced glossy magazines full of adverts and propaganda put out by the club to fool you, the fan, into thinking all is well.

Q

QPR: West London club eternally in the shadow of the other west London club, Brentford. Oh, and Chelsea. Short name, short attention span. Play at Loftus Road.

R

Ran: Slang term meaning to chase after (as in 'We ran them ragged'). Can also mean to run away (as in 'We ran like fuck').

Referee: The man in black on the pitch. Responsible for making sure that the game flows smoothly and the rules are adhered to. Ably assisted by two linesmen (see referee's assistant), all three of them should be subjected to a constant barrage of abuse. Even if they're having a good game, although this will be rare.

Referee's Assistant: The 'new' name for linesmen, it came into use as a result of political correctness and the appearance of female officials. Therefore, no true geezer should ever utter this name at all and always refer to them as 'linesman', 'wanker' or 'oi! you bald cunt!'

Replica Kits: Cynical rip-off designed to relieve football fans of their hard-earned money.

S

Sads: Ex-geezers who take their kids to football while wishing they were still 18 and single. To be treated with the utmost respect as, eventually, all geezers will become one (some sooner than others).

Scarfers: Another name for anoraks.

Scottish Football: See non-league football (with the possible exception of Rangers and Celtic who, if they had their way, would play in England anyway). Only useful for filling up the pools coupons.

Scouting: An activity done by people (usually wannabe geezers) who are looking for visiting groups of hooligans so that the two groups can get together for fisticuffs.

Seaman (David): Current England and Arsenal goalkeeper. Famous for so many vital saves over the years but the penalty stop against Scotland during Euro '96 stands head and shoulders above the rest.

Shankly (Bill): Scottish bloke who died years ago. Former Liverpool manager renowned for his caustic wit and responsible for making the scouse team of the '70s into one of the greatest sides ever known. Must be spinning in his grave now.

Shearer (Alan): Newcastle and England centre forward. Often said to be a bit of a boring bloke and renowned for being a very physical player or, if you support any club other then Newcastle United, a dirty fucking cheating bastard. Except when he plays for England, however, when he is a top bloke.

Sheffield United: The best club in Sheffield. I only say that because a good friend of mine supports them and he'll get the right hump if I say anything else. Play at Bramall Lane.

Sheffield Wednesday: The other club in Sheffield. Most famous for being supported by Roy Hattersley. Nothing else, really. Play at Hillsborough.

Six-O-Six: (Also known as *606*) BBC Radio Five football phone-in show on Saturday evenings. Not as good as it used to be as it is now hosted by David Mellor.

Skinner (Frank): Professional 'celebrity' fan. The other half of the so-called comedy duo Skinner and Baddiel (see Skinner and Baddiel). Makes great play of his apparent 'support' for West Brom and uses this as a comedy tool. This does not endear him to West Brom fans who, generally speaking, think he is a wanker.

Skinner and Baddiel: Professional 'blokes'. Widely regarded as a pair of tossers because of their role in both *Fantasy Football League* and the new-breed anthem 'Three Lions'.

Sky Television: Boo hiss. The one single reason why Premier League, FA Cup or international games are moved away from the traditional Saturday afternoons. As a result, all true football fans hate it and blame it for everything, but still watch it. Armchairs worship it.

Soccer: What wankers and new-breeds call football.

Soccer AM: Saturday morning footie programme on Sky Sports. Tragically, what is a great show is devoid of any credibility as it is hosted by a bird. This makes it perfect for armchairs and anathema for geezers.

Sorting Out (as in 'by West Ham fans'): Giving or receiving a good thumping for some reason or other.

Southampton: The top club down on the south coast, which is not much of a compliment. Most famous for keeping hold of Matt Le Tissier (see Le Tissier) for ages. Play at The Dell, which is a really crap ground.

Southend United: The Essex giants. Doomed for a lifetime of failure. If you live within 50 miles, do what everyone else does and watch West Ham. Play at Roots Hall.

Spank: Meaning to thump or slap, as in 'We gave them a spanking'.

Specials: Trains used to ferry football fans around in the golden days. A real laugh to be on, as most of the journeys were spent fighting with the other compartments, throwing things out of the window and wrecking the carriages. For some reason the police and British Rail stopped them. Can't think why.

Sport (The): Tabloid newspaper owned by the same bloke who owns Birmingham City. Most famous for having more naked breasts on show than all the other papers added together and multiplied by a factor of ten. Less well known for excellent footie coverage. Compulsory reading on any away trip.

Steam: Slang term used by hooligans meaning to attack another group of fans (as in 'We steamed into them'). Can also mean to smell (as in 'That bog's steaming').

Stewards: People inside and outside grounds wearing brightly coloured bibs or jackets. Stewards are supposedly responsible for security and safety inside grounds and are usually graduates of the 'Jobsworth' school of charm and good manners.

Stoke City: Club from just off the M6 in Staffordshire. Recently most famous for being supported by 'celebrity fan' Nick Hancock rather than their football, which says it all really. Play at The Britannia Stadium.

Sun (The): Tabloid newspaper famous for page three birds. Not popular in Liverpool or Graham Taylor's house, for different reasons.

Sunderland: Huge club from the north-east now back in the big time largely thanks to the efforts of their centre forward, who slunk out of Watford after failing to sign a new contract even though we had paid his wages throughout a very long lay-off due to a serious injury. There's bloody loyalty for you. Oh yes, and also famous for massive support and the legendary Roker Roar, a tradition that has continued even though they now play at The Stadium of Shite, I mean Light.

Swansea City: Another Welsh club. Like their good mates in

Cardiff (joke!), they are also known for their hatred of everything English.

Swindon Town: Snigger, snigger.

T

Talk Radio: Phone-in radio station providing only viable alternative to Radio Five and *606* on Saturdays. The place where Danny Baker works (see Baker).

Tarbuck (Jimmy): Scouse comic best known for the catchphrase 'Ho-ho!'.

Taylor (Graham): Former England football manager, all-round genius and bona fide top man. Made Watford Football Club great and then left. Recently returned to Vicarage Road and has started the process all over again. Winning the Division Two Championship on the last day of the 1997–98 season has certainly helped.

Terraces: The places where all the geezers stood and watched their football from back in the golden days. That was until the clubs decided to stick seats on them and double the prices overnight. Can still be found down in the lower leagues.

Tilbury Town: Non-league side from Essex known as the Dockers due to their close proximity to Tilbury Docks. My father-in-law drinks in their social club. No, really, he does.

Tranmere Rovers: Fifth club in Merseyside after Liverpool, Everton and their respective reserve sides. Disliked by me because of their involvement with John Aldridge, but that's a long story.

Transit Van: Made by Ford of Dagenham and used for everything from milk floats to bank robberies. Perfect vehicle for travelling to away games with groups of other geezers, as the minibus version carries up to 15 and the van takes up to 40! The good old tranny is also a favourite form of transport for the Old Bill on match days, and so if you are the cowardly type one should always be kept in sight.

Top Boy: Term meaning the leader of a hooligan firm (as in 'He's Top Boy').

Top Man: Term meaning a good bloke (as in 'He's a top man'). Is also the name of a high-street clothes shop but not one any self-respecting geezer would be seen dead in.

Tottenham Hotspur (also known as Spurs): North London club suffering from delusions of long-gone greatness and living in the shadow of Arsenal. Currently infested with Baldrick syndrome (as in 'I have a cunning plan'). Play at White Hart Lane.

V

Vaughan (Johnny): Host of Channel Four television show *The Big Breakfast*, true Chelsea fan and all-round top geezer. Indeed, probably the best example of the ilk to be found anywhere within the media.

W

Wannabe: Name for someone who wants to be something they are not and probably never will be, for example a good player or a decent manager. Can also be used as a term for people who 'wannabe' geezers or, alternatively, blokes without any kind of class or style. The types who, although one of the more vocal elements inside grounds, live in their replica shirts, read fanzines and bring musical instruments into stadia.

Watford: Glorious team known as 'The Hornets' or 'The 'Orns'. Supported by me and managed by the legendary Graham Taylor, so we are clearly destined for a return to greatness. Celebrity fans include Elton John and Ginger Spice, who are both to be applauded for their extremely good taste. Play at Vicarage Road.

Welsh Football: See non-league football and then think worse than that. Think about it: Wrexham, Cardiff and Swansea play in the English league, and they're crap. Imagine what the rest are like!

Wembley: Shit-hole home of the national side and where they play the FA Cup final, amongst other things.

West Bromwich Albion: Midlands club nicknamed 'The Baggies' for some odd reason and, like most clubs in that region, suffering from 'sleeping giant' syndrome. West Brom, as they are more commonly known, are also afflicted with 'That wanker Frank Skinner supports us' disease, although it is generally believed that as soon as football becomes less trendy this will cure itself.

West Ham United: The pride of east London and known as The Irons or The Hammers. Almost exclusively supported by geezers and not a place to visit for those of a nervous disposition. Used to be renowned for finding players who lived within spitting distance of the ground but now renowned for finding them within flying distance of Heathrow Airport. Play at Upton Park.

When Saturday Comes: Glorified fanzine aimed directly at, and written by, anally retentive armchairs and new-breeds. If you like to read about such 'interesting' subjects as the tactical naïvety of some arse-wipe Bolivian second division side, this is the magazine for you. Need I say any more?

Wimbledon: The one single team you do not want your team to play if the fixture is in any way significant. Unless you're Everton (allegedly). Once home of the infamous 'Crazy Gang', now home to various has-beens and wannabes. Sadly, the ending of the dream is only a matter of time now. Like Crystal Palace, play at Selhurst Park (and for quite how long is that going to be allowed to continue?).

Wolverhampton Wanderers: Black Country club currently in a coma somewhere in the Midlands. Great ground, great fans, shit team. Spot the problem! Play at Molineux.

Women's Football: Contradiction in terms or sarcastic reference to L*t*n T*wn. 'Played', if that's the right word, by geezer-birds and lesbians.

Z

Zulu Army: Large hooligan firm who follow Birmingham City FC. Best known for being incredibly noisy inside grounds and incredibly noisy outside grounds. Not a favourite group of the Old Bill.

Epilogue

Some people who read this book may think that the bigoted, sexist and abusive world of the geezer no longer exists, the character I describe a parody of a lifestyle no longer relevant to the caring, sharing '90s. They will spout on about the growth in popularity of the game, the explosion of Sky Television, the Lord Justice Taylor Report and even the rise of women's football. And, as they talk, they will turn to political correctness and anti-sexism and will say that all of this change has been good for the game. That every single word written here belongs back in the dark ages of the '70s and '80s when the culture I describe spent the majority of its time attempting to destroy both football and itself. But they are the type of people who sit in directors' boxes or watch the game on television or from behind the windows of executive suites. And they are wrong.

Football is all about passion. It can be a few small kids in a council park or 22 internationals at Wembley Stadium, but the same ideal is there: to win. And with that ideal comes emotion and fervour and intensity. The higher up the football ladder you go, the greater those feelings get, and at the very top, not only do those who play the game experience them, but so do those who watch it. Combine those experiences and passions and you get the one thing that sets football apart from every other sport in the world: atmosphere. Of course, atmosphere can be found everywhere, from the cinema to the local greyhound stadium, but at football it's different. At football you get a kind of atmosphere you will not find anywhere else because it contains two unique elements: frustration and anger. Frustration that we weren't good enough to be out there playing, and anger aimed at those who have come to take our dream of victory away from us.

But it isn't football fans who create that atmosphere, it's men, or, to be more specific, geezers. Any crowd can make a noise, sing a song or applaud when someone does something worthy. That isn't what I'm talking about. I'm talking about something almost tangible. Something that makes your hair stand on end and that you can almost grab hold of because it is so electric. Geezers do that. No one else. And they are certainly not in the past, nor are they an invention or a comic creation. If you walk into any ground in the country and spend your time watching the crowd as opposed to the actual game, you will see them. Not just the odd one or two, but hundreds, and they will be everywhere. The geezer is not the '70s or '80s, he's right now. And he's an essential part of the game we call football. His game. And football needs him.

Yet while many of the new-breed football fans will condemn this chauvinist as a throwback, there are a couple of messages to be found in the fact that his type has continued to exist despite the best efforts of two generations of middle-class do-gooders. The first is that at some time in their lives all men need to act like this. They need to spend time in the company of other men and be brash, abusive and arrogant. They need to do things without thinking of the possible consequences and they need to face their fears and walk right through them. That is what men do. History has proven that and everyone should be thankful for it. Instead, in our everyday lives, those needs are being suppressed and we males are being told to get in touch with our feminine side. New man, soft man, are they really what everybody wants? A nation of Frank Skinners and Dale Wintons?

But on the terraces of Britain, those male appetites are still being fulfilled and the men who stand there are all the better for it. What's more, they know it as well, and that's why they do what they do.

Just as importantly, the geezers have survived because football owes them a great debt. It wasn't the corporate boys who kept football going when it was unfashionable, nor was it some hooray Henry who drove to Carlisle on a wet Tuesday night in 1981; it was a geezer. Oh yes, you can argue that it was the geezers and the hooligans who almost destroyed the game through their activities and, to be honest, there is some truth in that. But that wasn't the only reason for football's decline. The game had been bled dry for years and all of a sudden it became just another entertainment. It couldn't compete with the cinema or television and so it started to go down the pan. But the geezers kept going and they were the ones who kept it afloat. Football knew that, and that's why it has always left them alone.

Yet by continuing to take them for granted, football is playing a dodgy game. The explosion of the big-screen culture, so prevalent in pubs throughout Britain, is already providing an attractive alternative to games where ticket prices and inflation seem to go hand-in-hand. Why pay top whack for a seat amongst a horde of school kids and new-breeds when you can watch the game in a pub full of geezers for nothing? And don't for one second think the atmosphere isn't as good, either. That's where the atmosphere has gone.

And that is the real danger facing football as we move towards the end of the century. Because when the new-breeds discover ice hockey or ten-pin bowling and the City boys pull out all their money because the game has become less fashionable, the geezers will not be there to pick up the pieces. Not this time. We'll all be down the pub. Because that's where they sold our game.

Up the 'Ornets.

Like all the books I have ever been involved with, this one would not have been possible without the help and support of football supporters everywhere.

If you have any views on the content, or have a story to tell about an experience you have either enjoyed or suffered during your lifetime of football fandom, be it funny, sad, tragic or even downright bizarre, please write to me at:

PO BOX 766
HEMEL HEMPSTEAD
HP1 2TU

All correspondence will be treated with the utmost confidentiality.